PRAISE FOR *THE BLEEDING EDGE*

"Bill Raduchel is a pioneer of the digital revolution. The deeply instructive stories in this book are much more than a compulsively readable personal history. They're a master class in how to succeed in the business of technology." —**Eric Schmidt,** former CEO, Google, and co-author of *The New Digital Age*

"For more than half a century, Bill Raduchel has been the Zelig of the tech world—somehow involved in nearly everything and knowing everyone. This book should be required reading for anyone thinking about a career in tech." —**Steve Case,** cofounder and former CEO, AOL, and author of the *New York Times* bestseller *The Third Wave*

"Bill has been my thesis advisor, dorm advisor, economics professor, mentor, CXO, friend, and co-worker since 1973. At Sun for over a decade, he helped us take revenue from $1 billion to $14 billion. He steered us through a financial crisis in 1989 and was in the middle of every major deal and innovation. *The Bleeding Edge* gives a perspective on management and change that is unique. He was there. He lived and helped formulate it." —**Scott McNealy,** co-founder and former CEO, Sun Microsystems

"I hired Bill to advise the Daily Mail and General Trust because of his long experience in technology and media. As this book shows, he's also a shrewd judge of people and the systems that make companies successful." —**Jonathan Harmsworth,** 4th Viscount Rothermere and chairman of Daily Mail and General Trust

"Few in the tech world are as accomplished and as deeply embedded in its firmament as Bill Raduchel. *The Bleeding Edge* is more than just a memoir—it's a mini-MBA, a computer science degree, and a front-row-seat history of the digital revolution all rolled into one must-read book." **—Christopher A. Smith,** author of *Privacy Pandemic* and digital security expert

"Bill Raduchel's memoir is about being a witness to change. His sixty years at the center of technology's transformation of culture put him inside the boardrooms of Data Resources, Sun Microsystems, Apple, and AOL Time Warner, where he helped shape how the Internet would change our lives. Reading this book is like being a wallflower listening in on the extraordinary conversations of gifted visionaries: Steve Case, Bill Gates, Scott McNealy, and Steve Jobs. Wise, funny, always perceptive, and a thoroughly enjoyable read." **—Paul Vidich,** former executive vice president of global digital strategy, Warner Music Group

"A fascinating after-action report by a perceptive player at the highest levels in three major corporations—Xerox, Sun Microsystems, and AOL—as they struggled with the evolving demands of the digital revolution." **—Roger Levien,** former vice president of strategy, Xerox

THE
BLEEDING
EDGE

www.amplifypublishinggroup.com

The Bleeding Edge: My Six Decades at the Forefront of the Tech Revolution

For more information, please contact:
Amplify Publishing, an imprint of Amplify Publishing Group
620 Herndon Parkway, Suite 220
Herndon, VA 20170
info@amplifypublishing.com

Library of Congress Control Number: 2023909243
CPSIA Code: PRV0623A
ISBN-13: 978-1-63755-829-4
Printed in the United States

TO MY PARENTS, WHO GAVE ME MY VALUES,

AND MY PROFESSORS WHO SET MY DIRECTION:

KEN ALEXANDER, WALTER ADAMS, HENRY ROSOVSKY,

HOLLIS CHENERY, ARTHUR SMITHIES, AND JOHN KENNETH GALBRAITH.

BILL RADUCHEL

THE BLEEDING EDGE

MY SIX DECADES AT THE FOREFRONT OF THE TECH REVOLUTION

From Scott McNealy to Steve Jobs to Steve Case
to Steve Ballmer and Other Titans
of Technology and Media

amplify
an imprint of Amplify Publishing Group

CONTENTS

WALKING WITH GIANTS

TED TURNER WAS ALWAYS LARGER THAN LIFE TO ME for his incredible foresight to see how satellites would transform the television industry (I still remember waiting for the first satellite TV signal to be broadcast) and capitalize on it with the creation of Turner Broadcasting and CNN. He was—and is—a giant.

I first met Ted at the World Economic Forum at Davos in 1986, where he bumped me from giving a talk on the future of paper to a group of media moguls. The moguls were only interested in him. I understood why.

Now, on January 10, 2000 (almost fifteen years later), he was walking in front of me as we entered the press conference for what at the time was perhaps the biggest moment in the history of media—the AOL–Time Warner merger. In the 1990s, going online was almost synonymous with America Online—predating Amazon for shopping, Facebook for mass messaging, and Google for email.

The internet was only six years old, yet hearing the phrase "You've got mail" was ubiquitous. There were competitors: Prodigy (a joint venture of IBM and Sears), Microsoft, Earthlink, CompuServe, and others, but AOL was by far the leader. Combining with Time Warner's massive reach with brands like CNN, HBO, *Sports Illustrated, People* magazine, and of course Warner Brothers would place the new company in an unprecedented position of industry dominance.

"We are literally transforming the landscape of media and communications in the new millennium, a time we think of as the Internet Century," said AOL CEO Steve Case, who had brought me into AOL only a few months earlier as chief technology officer to help craft their broadband future. Case and Time Warner CEO Jerry Levin were, of course, two other legends of the time—Case for pioneering the concept of online media and Levin for recognizing that media would become an online industry in the new century.

The press conference was really a strange event. We had already made the public announcement about the merger. From that point on the companies had to operate separately until antitrust clearance was achieved. No one could say much more than what was in the public text—but everyone was looking for clues.

Ted was in a great mood. He commented to the person next to him that he had made $1 billion in the deal and wistfully wondered whether Jane would come back (Jane Fonda had recently divorced him). I was less ebullient about the $180 billion deal—for reasons that I'll explain later—though the potential for greatness was there. Ted would later calculate that he lost nearly $8 billion (80 percent of his wealth) on the merger and compare it to the disasters of the wars in Vietnam and Afghanistan. And of course, Jane never came back.*

In the afterglow of the announcement, I got to spend more time with Ted. He was an incredibly gracious host when we visited Turner Broadcasting headquarters in Atlanta. A trip to his baseball stadium was epic. We saw things the public would never see. I learned some tricks of his management style, such as starting a meeting ten minutes early to be done by the stated time. You were not late to a meeting with Ted Turner.

Along the way, I found myself wondering how I got there, in the company of legends like Ted, Steve, and Jerry—and calling them all by their first names.

How did this happen? How did a middle-class kid from a tiny town near Lake Superior in the Upper Peninsula of Michigan get to be the CTO of what promised to be the leading media company of the era?

---

*   Arango, Tim, "How the AOL-Time Warner Merger Went So Wrong," *New York Times*, January 10, 2020, https://www.nytimes.com/2010/01/11/business/media/11merger.html.

THE BLEEDING EDGE

ROM THE MOMENT I FIRST SAW A COMPUTER, in 1961 at the age of fifteen, I've been fascinated by technology and how it could revolutionize our world, as I was certain it would. Over the ensuing decades, I had the immense privilege of living and working at the bleeding edge—a term coined to describe technology so new and advanced that it is still unproven and perhaps unpredictable—of that revolution.

That journey began with my work as an economist and statistician at Harvard, where I used my time to teach myself computer science. It was a world dominated by the IBM 029 Key Punch—a bulky, completely ridiculous machine by today's standards, but state-of-the-art at the time.

I look back at that era with wonder. I spent up to 100 hours a week for years sitting at the keypunch writing software. And I loved it. You could "program" the 029 with a punch card attached to a drum, and I became an expert. It was amazing how much you could do with it.

Computing worked like this: You assembled a "job" in cardboard boxes of meticulously ordered 80-column punch

IMB 029 Key Punch (1960)

cards and submitted it over a counter to a team of operators. You then waited for your job to be completed, as the computer could only run one job at a time. The only way to use the computer was through these punch cards; the results came in the form of more punch cards or a printout from a 144-column IBM line printer.

Harvard got one of the first disk drives installed by IBM. It looked like a two-door refrigerator. Total storage was five megabytes. (The smallest iPhone model sold today offers 128,000 megabytes.) Nevertheless, it was game-changing—now information could live between jobs. It had one minor problem: if you gave it the correct sequence of commands, the drive would "dance" on the floor, which was not good for the machine but irresistible to the programmers.

I was not the only one spending my time at the keypunch. My office mate, David Packard, once wrote a 6,000-line program at the keypunch in IBM 7094 assembly language that ran perfectly the first time. We were a small, motley crew—even at Harvard. However, we were pushing the state of the art and using computers for things no one had contemplated.

I created statistical and modeling software that again tested boundaries. Literally hundreds of copies of that software found their way around the world. One program allowed economists to process orders of magnitude more data than any other, and at least one won a Nobel Prize in part as a result. I wrote software for a friend to analyze the Terman data in ways no one else had, although we were stumped by the need to look at the color of the notation on the card, as we had a copy without markings. I was a constant thorn in the side of the computing center staff and their IBM support team when I found things that did not work right.

Timesharing was a revolutionary idea: sit at a terminal and interact with a shared computer. By the mid-1970s, Harvard had a timesharing computer, but it really did not do what I needed it to do. I only played with it.

But Harvard also gave me the opportunity to teach with the legendary economist John Kenneth Galbraith in his course on his book *The New Industrial State*. When he retired in 1975 I created my own course, Computers and Society. Most of the social issues we have with technology today are unchanged from the 1970s. I explored these issues and others in my book (named in homage to Galbraith) *The New Technology State*.

I left Harvard with an appreciation for what software could do and how computers worked. That appreciation was enhanced during my time at IDA, the Institute for Defense Analyses. When I started working with Data Resources, Inc. in the late 1970s I acquired my own teletype terminal, into which I placed a handset to connect over phone lines.

Again—fifty years ago that was the state of the art. When I got it, I felt so privileged. Over time, these terminals got smaller and more portable, and for years I lugged one around. It was the size of a suitcase, but it only provided access to a mainframe that in total had a fraction of the power of the smartphone in your hand today.

Data Resources at the time was the largest non-governmental distributor of economic data and modeling software in the world—for the first time I found myself with a full-time job on the bleeding edge of the computer revolution. I also began to see its enormous commercial potential.

The Burroughs computers we used at DRI were the most advanced that anyone had for time- sharing at the time, and

Teletype Model 33 (1963)

no one else offered an information service over timesharing. We had telephone lines all over the world coming back to our data center in Lexington, Massachusetts. In modern parlance, we were a cloud for our customers. People came to see us, including Bob Metcalf (who invented Ethernet) and Larry Ellison (who founded Oracle).

It was clear that personal computers posed an existential threat to the business of DRI, so I started tracking them closely. From the early days of Esther Dyson's PC Forum I was always in attendance, and I met all the players of that nascent industry. There was such energy and optimism. I was largely a bystander in those meetings, but it was fascinating to hear from, for example, Ben Rosen, who funded Compaq, and Philip Don Estridge, the first leader of the IBM PC division. Tragically, Don died in a Delta Airlines crash in Dallas. As part of DRI's DataKits project, I spent a lot of time with Dan Fylstra and Dan Bricklin at VisiCorp, who created and sold the first successful spreadsheet for Apple II personal computers. Unintentionally, I funded development of the software which became Lotus 1-2-3 as part of our DRILink project, which also taught me a lot about Unix and the basics of a computer system. We sold Unix microcomputers from a variety of companies, including Onyx. Onyx was run by Doug Broyles, who hired Scott McNealy to run his operations on my recommendation. Scott, of course, went on to become a co-founder of Sun Microsystems. One of my other projects at DRI was analyzing whether graphical user interfaces would win. That seems so quaint now.

In the early 1980s, the CEO of McGraw-Hill—now known mostly for educational publishing, but which had many other business information services at the time—wanted to be the first in the world to provide online information to businesses, a process he jumpstarted by buying DRI. That too kept me on the bleeding edge.

We bought Monchik-Weber, the most innovative supplier of trading data to Wall Street, and discussed leveraging that into the home with John Malone at TCI. We almost bought Borland Software, led by Philippe Kahn, which acquisition died because of a story on toga parties in the *Wall Street Journal* the day the board of directors was to have approved it. More on that later . . .

We opened the first online trading service for oil futures. We met with Bill Gates. We went to Cupertino to a meeting with Steve Jobs, but were told he was not in the building and to leave. While we waited for a car back to the airport, our division CEO encountered Jobs in the men's room; he offered no apology or explanation.

My next stop was Xerox as part of the corporate staff working for the CEO and chief staff officer. After my first meeting with the head of the systems division, he went back to his headquarters and told his staff they could not lie anymore to corporate. I was in many ways the one-eyed man in the land of the blind.

It is very hard to change corporate DNA, even though Xerox tried hard to do so. I was the corporate IT strategist, and Xerox had invented most of the office technologies we use even today. I ended up as the chief product officer for the office systems business, which I closed down in a customer-friendly way.

I learned a lot about multiprocessing by licensing Sun Microsystems the patents that formed the core of its server strategy, again completely on the bleeding edge. The "snoopy buss" covered by those patents was fundamental to the success of Sun. There was a little professional awkwardness in that I represented both Sun and Xerox, but I did so with the full knowledge of both parties.

In the late 1980s, I moved to Sun Microsystems as the corporate planner and "deal guy." I served in that capacity for over a decade, as well as various times as chief financial officer, chief information officer, vice president of human resources, and chief strategy officer. I also managed our relationships with our major Japanese partners: Fujitsu, Toshiba, C. Itoh, Sony, and Sega. These were all at the CEO level except for Ken Kutaragi, the creator of the Sony Playstation, who always worked independently. Early on, I negotiated a potential deal with Microsoft with Steve Ballmer, a former student of mine, but our respective CEOs did not agree. I did multiple deals (or attempted deals) with Steve Jobs, and negotiated the 1995 acquisition of Apple by Sun, which we brought to conclusion but then passed on. I later negotiated with Steve on a potential acquisition of NeXT. My last major deal was the partnership with AOL, which gave Sun access to and eventual ownership of all the server-side software technology of Netscape.

That deal eventually got me to AOL, where one of my first acts was making their Gecko browser open source, which created Mozilla and Firefox. In June of 2001, *InfoWorld* named me their chief technology officer of the year, saying that I was going to redefine the home entertainment experience. That was the plan at the time, but it never happened (you'll find out why in the chapter on my time at AOL Time Warner).

As I look back, that was probably the public peak of my career, and it comprises the longest chapter of this book. We, AOL, bought Time Warner in early 2000. AOL had 55 percent of the equity in the final company, so although it was a "merger of equals," AOL shareholders theoretically had control—though it did not turn out that way. In both companies, I was on the bleeding edge again, trying to figure out where technology and media were going. I was the strategist supporting Steve Case; when he was forced out, my time was up shortly thereafter. Patents on digital streaming where I was the lead inventor went on to be acquired by Microsoft and then Facebook, now Meta.

At AOL I met Sean Parker, who was the co-founder of Napster, though he had left Napster by the time I met him. I could tell immediately how smart he was. Sean taught me what social media could be. Through Sean, I met the Facebook team early on (though I had a dinner with Mark Zuckerberg through another pathway). Through pure serendipity, the night the Facebook news feed went live, I cooked dinner for Sean, which was interrupted many times by pages from Mark, so I heard that debate live.

At the invitation of Paul Vidich of Warner Music, I was at the seminal meeting with Steve Jobs that launched licensed music on iTunes. I made a key contribution to the contract by defining what a "device" was as opposed to a "computer." On a device, the user has no access to the file system, a restriction that resulted in the architecture for the AppStore. I had numerous similar conversations with the Warner Brothers team as they figured out their internet strategy. Jim Chiddix, who invented most of modern cable architecture, was a great teacher.

In the early 2000s, I was involved in the evolution of the internet on phones as chairman of Opera Software. When the iPhone was introduced, the number one browser in the world on phones was Opera Mini, which was in reality a proxy service in Iceland. Opera itself was a player in the browser wars, but not the winner—though it could have been had it been willing to take the terms Google offered. I eventually pushed them into mobile advertising, which was a success.

These stories and more await you in the chapters ahead— my personal journey, which I hope illuminates in some small way the story of how technology has profoundly transformed our world.

CHAPTER 1

THE MAKINGS OF ME (1946–1966)

WE ARE ALL SHAPED BY OUR LIFE EXPERIENCES, especially the experiences of our youth. I am no exception. As a child in the 40s and 50s, my family and I were stalwarts of the Grace Methodist Church in Houghton, Michigan. One of the members liked me, and she used to bake me bread. Not just any bread, but a particular wheat germ bread I loved. She and her husband lived a simple, inelegant life. She used coffee cans for bread pans. The bread was round, and I loved it.

Her husband was known for his frugality. He worked as an accountant and would walk home along the street where I lived. He would collect twigs that had fallen from trees to take home and use as fuel. When his wife became ill and needed transport home from a distant hospital, my father drove her. She clearly needed an ambulance, but the husband said he could not afford it. I was a passenger on that trip.

She did not make it, and for the rest of his life the husband put a rose on her grave every day. Rain or shine.

Blizzard or hail. Every day. I watched him crawl over six-foot snowbanks to get into the cemetery. I admired him for it, though at ten I wondered why.

When he died several years later, it turned out he was not poor. Indeed, by the standards of the early 1950s he was rich. He hated paying taxes, so he left his one daughter the most he could without triggering estate tax. The bulk of his money went to support historically Black colleges in the South, his wife's deeply felt concern.

I took a very great lesson away from this: try to live your life without regrets. Regrets are the worst thing to accumulate. We all accumulate some, but to this day I try to do things for others when I can, because there may not be time in the future.

I learned the same lesson from my father, who was always doing things for other people. He was the informal town advisor. He served on the village council for years. He promised my mother he would step down one year and did not run for re-election. The phone rang on election night, and he had been re-elected on write-in votes. My mother gave up. We moved away for two years, and he was elected anew in the first election after we returned. He served twenty years as the chairman of Local Board 32 of the Selective Service System, a thankless role.

My father fought to bring cable television to town early. There were not a lot of stations available (this was long before satellites). I am the rare American who grew up on Canadian television. I watched the *National News* for some time before I understood it was the Canadian news. I was seven.

As I entered seventh grade, my father was transferred

from Houghton to Rhinelander, Wisconsin. However, almost as soon as we got there, his employer, Mobil Oil, informed him that all employees over forty-five were being let go as a cost-reduction strategy (legal then), so we knew we would be returning to Houghton. We started living a two-location life. That meant I never really integrated into my class there, though I had good friends.

I lost my father when I was fourteen, but honestly my memories are faded now. What I do remember is his funeral. I was at the funeral home, but as I was a boy, I was in the back room. Some neighbors arrived and asked to see me, so I came out. Sitting there were the local representatives to Congress, both state legislators, the mayors of both towns, and many of the council members. I was impressed already, but then the firemen from the area came in uniform to show their respects. I was moved. Shortly thereafter, all the local taxi drivers arrived. I cried.

The breadth and sincerity of the people at that funeral home left an indelible impression on me. All my life, I have tried to emulate my father in respecting all people regardless of status or stature.

My next great lesson came from my first boss. At sixteen, the minimum age to work in Michigan, I became a doorman at the Lode Theater—a job I held for the next five years. Starting pay was 45 cents an hour, but Hilda always paid you at 50 cents an hour on your first paycheck. If you told her about the error, you kept your job and your rate. If you did not, well, you were not there long. I wrote about Hilda on *Fast Company* nearly thirty years ago, and to this day every week that story reappears on LinkedIn or Twitter.

The lesson—taking your first job is hiring your first boss.*

We were the Sputnik generation. I still remember the panic that ensued when the Soviet Union launched the first satellite. I heard the news on the car radio on a Sunday afternoon drive (yes, people did that). The result was that getting the country smarter, faster in the sciences became critical, so along with many others I was jumped a grade in math and science classes. That meant I was again between two worlds, as I had two sets of classmates. To this day I identify with the class ahead of me, because it was with them that I spent most of my time. I was a bit of a geek, and I cannot say high school was the best time of my life.

I was invited into the Joe Berg Copper Country Science Seminar, which met weekly at Michigan Tech, the local college. Thence I was sent to a six-week summer program at Northern Michigan University, one hundred miles away. It was my first time away from home. My father had died the preceding fall, so this was a big deal for me. At NMU I was exposed to modern mathematics and, importantly, to computers. My first computer exposure was to the vacuum-tube monster that fired Nike anti-aircraft missiles. I was fifteen. I actually got to use an IBM 1620 with 10,000 characters of memory (weirdly, it was a decimal machine), and I learned to program in the new language Fortran—but I don't remember doing anything meaningful.

My senior year of high school was mainly spent at

---

* Muoio, Anna, "How to Make Your Career Move," *Fast Company*, October/ November 1997, https://www.fastcompany.com/33076/how-make-your-career-move.

Michigan Tech. Michigan law required that I have four years of English to graduate high school, so I returned each school day for one hour for that class. I had decided to become a chemical engineer, so I was very busy at Tech. The next year, when I was full-time, I had forty-three hours of instruction each week, not counting homework. While I did well in the engineering classes, one professor, Ken Alexander, got me excited about economics, so I took a lot of social science.

A former neighbor, Hank Berry, looked out for me and landed me a job at the Institute for Mineral Research on campus. There I wrote my first academic paper, "The Effect of Temperature on the Zeta Potential." I remember little of that paper. Most of my time was spent as a research assistant to Adnan Goksol, who was studying fly ash, the tiny specs of carbon that come out of a smokestack. My job was what would be a Google search today: I went to the library forty hours a week with a stack of index cards and read back issues of journals looking for articles on fly ash. When I found one, I filled out an index card. Google search is a lot more efficient.

However, the Institute gave me backdoor access to computers. The first was a Bendix G15, the first transistor computer. The only way to communicate with it was via paper tape, though some creative people used its bell to send out Morse code signals. It was more for curiosity than purpose. There was another IBM 1620 where I could write Fortran, though I did a few tasks using absolute machine language. I did a few things that seem trivial today but seemed magical to the people for whom I was doing the work. That was the extent of my computer experience.

IBM 1620 (1959)

My senior year was spent at Michigan State University in East Lansing. I thought about switching to computer science, but found out I already knew more than was being taught in the senior classes, so I stayed in economics. With help from Walter Adams, one of MSU's iconic professors and one-time acting president, I was able to graduate in one year and head off to graduate school. I really had little appreciation for what schools I could reach, so I applied to Harvard, Yale, Michigan, Harvard Law, and Northwestern Law.

All accepted me, though Michigan offered no scholarship assistance. Money had been scarce as an undergraduate. I was a Thomas J. Watson Memorial Merit Scholar, sponsored by IBM, which paid my undergraduate expenses, but beyond the basics I paid for the rest myself. My job at the movie theater taught me to be a projectionist, which funded my time at MSU; summers I had the Google search job. Graduate school seemed like nirvana.

CHAPTER 2

HARVARD UNIVERSITY (1966–1977)

T WASN'T NIRVANA, BUT HARVARD WAS CERTAINLY TRANS-FORMATIONAL. I still remember my forlorn feelings when I was dropped off by taxi in front of the graduate school dormitory. I had just taken my first real airplane flight and my first taxi ride by myself. It was dark, and the dormitory was far from inviting. Oxford Hall was old. The rooms were large but shared. The bathrooms were one per floor. The best thing was that we had a daily maid service. It would be my home for the next two years. Things got better when my roommate, Herb Wang, arrived. Herb had a car.

Harvard had the best economics department in the country at that time, and I admit I was a little surprised that I was admitted. I was a huge beneficiary of standardized tests; without them, I was just a decent student from a small, rural town and would have become a chemical engineer. Instead, I got great educations at great universities. I later learned that my class was very different than past classes in economics, because the new chair of the economics department, Henry Rosovsky, had decided to admit based on academic merit regardless of undergraduate institution. I may have been the first ever admitted from Michigan State. Two classmates were from Iowa State!

My first year at Harvard was pedestrian. However, in the second year, I became the research assistant to Marc Nerlove, who was then visiting from the University of Chi-cago. That is when

Bendix G15 (1956)

I began to turn from economics and statistics to computer science—albeit all self-taught. Nerlove was studying birth rates in Puerto Rico. Despite all our work, his model failed to accurately predict them. He finally found the issue when he went to visit the *municipo*, which was the most deviant from the model. Forced to spend the night due to a storm, he discovered a large freight train went through the town every morning at 4 a.m. and woke everyone up. Models predict based on the data provided, and no dataset had a variable for that.

At first the work was all bespoke, but eventually I tired of that and wrote software for general use to (properly) do the statistical analysis economists love. I was named a fellow of the Harvard Computing Center on the IBM Donation, along with David W. Packard, Jr. (he of the 6,000-line keypunch, whose father co-founded Hewlett-Packard). The National Bureau of Economic Research funded my computer usage. I was terrible at documentation, so my friend Melinda Eads, whose husband also worked with Marc Nerlove, added a poem from Lewis Carroll to my "manual":

> The method I used I would gladly explain
> While I have it so clear in my head
> If I had but the time and you had but the brain
> But much more remains to be said*

IBM 7094 (1960)

Software at this time was something you gave away. Software patents were not legal. So I gave it away. I have no idea how many copies were made or how many universities used it or for how long. In our own ways, we pushed the limits of the IBM 7094 Harvard had at the time.

---

* Carroll, Lewis, *The Hunting of the Snark: An Agony, in Eight Fits* (New York: Macmillan Co., 1899).

David worked on a complete concordance to the Roman historian Livy—an incredible accomplishment at the time. You can buy a used copy on Amazon today. We spent hours together at the keypunch writing code, usually in the post-midnight hours when computer turnaround was much faster. The turnaround time could be hours during the busy daytime shift, so the dedicated types like me worked the late nights. Turnaround could be almost instant at 3 a.m., especially if you brought the operators donuts and coffee.

David and I once spent two weeks in a contest to see who could write the fastest procedure to tell whether a word (computer memory unit) was a zero or a minus zero, which mattered a lot because a minus zero meant it was a missing value. It was a tie. He was faster for a zero and I for a minus zero.

Most economic models at the time were linear, but linear modeling is a poor approximation to the world outside of small changes. I pushed the envelope and did nonlinear models. This got me a summer job with the World Bank building a nonlinear model of the Mekong River Delta for the forthcoming post-war period that never came. I thought at the time that this research was purely academic. It was.

My own PhD thesis was a nonlinear model for development planning, which at the time was a booming field in economics. That was my home and sanctuary as an economist. I was sponsored by Hollis Chenery, who is probably most famous as the co-owner (with his sister) of two race horses, Secretariat and Riva Ridge. Hollis was incredibly good to me in so many ways. One thing he taught me was the importance of being able to read upside down and backwards so I could read everything on his desk when we met. He was a skilled bureaucrat.

One Tuesday, he told me he had to postpone our weekly Wednesday meeting to Thursday, because he had to go to Kentucky. He and his sister sold Secretariat prior to the running of his last race, and the buyers wanted a policy to cover their cost in case he was gay. The arcana of race horses was new to me, but Hollis went to Kentucky to meet with the Lloyds of London underwriter. As he explained to me on Thursday, the underwriter asked for thirty minutes alone with the horse, then quoted a fee of $250,000. Hollis asked him what he learned in that thirty minutes that allowed him to set the fee. After some mumbling, the underwriter admitted he made it up. Living in an academic world, it is good when the real world intrudes to bring you back to reality.

The Harvard Institute for International Development was the organization run by Chenery, and I had an office and a shared secretary. In 1972 I went to Korea for six weeks as part of a program sponsored by the country's president to get young Korean PhDs to return. He created the Korea Development Institute, which is still there and which is where I worked. I had a wonderful time and enjoyed meeting so many people. Because the president of Korea sponsored the program, my visa reflected that, so I was treated royally most of the time. It is good to be the personal guest of the dictator in a military dictatorship.

For my modeling work, I taught myself a lot of computer science along the way, but I learned a lot more helping a friend. Sam Rea, now dead, was one of my best friends in graduate school. He became a professor at the University of Toronto. He secured a $5,000 grant for me to help him write software to do his PhD thesis. He needed to do standard statistical analysis, but on hundreds of thousands of records. There was no existing software that could do that, and even if there was, standard techniques would have cost hundreds of thousands of dollars. I really believe in the minimal superset principle: never solve the problem itself but its minimal superset. That is what I did.

I set about writing SCORE: System Conceived for One-Pass Regression Estimation. Along the way, I taught myself how to write a compiler and a virtual machine. Most variables in these sorts of analyses are what are called dummy variables, either a 1 or a 0. Other software stored them as floating-point numbers, 1.0 or 0.0. Floating-point arithmetic is incredibly time-consuming relative to integer computing, and a 1 or 0 can be stored as a single bit, instead of a 32-bit floating-point number. I developed an algorithm to do that and published it in the peer-reviewed *Collected Algorithms of the Association for Computing Machinery*, as was the custom of the time. Overall, SCORE was ten to a hundred times more efficient and less costly and was not restricted in the number of observations it could handle. People ran more than a million records through it. Nobel Prizes followed.

When I was not promoted to associate professor at Harvard, I looked seriously at offers from the University of California at Berkeley and Michigan State University. However, in the end, for a mixture of personal and professional reasons, I accepted a position as director of freshman scholarships from Fred Jewett, then dean of admissions and financial aid for Harvard College. The Department of Economics made me a lecturer on economics, and I stayed on in a never-never land.

I continued to teach graduate econometrics, which is a

core course of the graduate program; it was unusual for this to be taught by someone without *professor* in their title. However, I did a good job (students have told me). It required my software and it was a lot of work, so no one else wanted to teach it. I still taught a section of Economics 10, the introductory course and largest on campus, and was the assistant to John Kenneth Galbraith in his class. When that ended, I taught Computers and Society, a course based on recommendations from the Association for Computing Machinery. For that course, I started studying the brain as a computer system. More people should. What we know is that creativity is a random permutation of our past. This is why diversity is so important when solving a new problem. The past which is tweaked may not seem related, but that does not matter.

Harvard got their money's worth out of me. Another of the many tasks I did was write exam questions for Economics 10. One year I asked students to discuss what happened if a monopolist sold through perfectly competitive resellers rather than directly. In theory, nothing. I think Steve Ballmer, later CEO of Microsoft, was in that year, and that question became the business model for Microsoft. I never asked Steve ... but that was their model. Surprisingly, the admissions job got me even more into computers. After the merger of the two admissions offices, I had a new title as the assistant dean of admissions and financial aid for research and data processing (the longest title in the university). I was also a lecturer on economics and a member of the Faculty of Arts and Sciences. I think at one point I had fourteen actual titles; having multiple titles was very common, but fourteen was a lot.

The entire admissions and financial aid process when I arrived was manual. In my spare time, I changed all that. I became a master of programming in PL-1. Within a year, we were able to reduce staff significantly and improve the process overall.

You can—and should!—read more about the Harvard admissions process in Appendix 1, which is an article that I wrote in 1978 and submitted to *Harvard Magazine*. They accepted it, but after a call from the dean of the Faculty of Arts and Sciences they asked me as a personal favor to withdraw it. I did.

After a year, the university decided to merge Harvard and Radcliffe admissions, and I did all the software and statistical analysis to make that happen. Key to making it happen was the random assignment of applicants to staff members to evaluate. Without that, trust would have been impossible. The former Radcliffe staff were friendly but apprehensive of me, but after a year we were great friends, helped in no small part by the fact that I doubled the number of women admitted from my areas.

But the Department of Economics had no use for my skills. The administration was no different. One assistant dean in particular thought I was overpaid. I was promised a promotion to be the registrar of Harvard College, which would have given me all the administrative software. Alas, it turned out they had the dates wrong, and the vacancy wouldn't open for five more years. The expectation was that I would just wait. That, and a feeling of having learned all I was going to learn there, motivated me to leave.

I wanted to leave on good terms. I accepted a position

at the Institute for Defense Analyses, where I had been a consultant for years and where I had an existing Top Secret security clearance. They were very flexible. I offered to stay at Harvard until the end of the academic year, but I wanted something close to market pay. I was given an emphatic no by the assistant dean who had to approve, so I left. Bill Fitzsimmons, now the dean of admissions but then the director of admissions, had hired a good person to succeed me, but he was not close to me in writing software. We overlapped for a few weeks, and then he was on his own.

Six weeks later Bill called me and asked me to rescue them. Remember that I was a lone wolf, though not by choice. The admissions software was probably only 50,000 lines or so, but that is a lot for one person. I asked for assistance, but it was never funded. I did not think I had been irresponsible. Anyway, for the next eighteen months I made frequent trips to Cambridge to keep the office running. I was paid decently, but it was a lot of effort.

I received distress calls for years from random people at multiple universities running some program I had written and forgotten. I tried to help, but the underlying systems had usually changed, so there was little I could do. All this taught me that software, which I admit I take for granted, is like magic to most people—and those people don't value it. If you don't understand something, I guess self-importance means you undervalue it. I watched this again and again as I went through my career.

I particularly enjoyed the time I spent with Galbraith, who was never a Nobel Prize winner but was frequently nominated. His landmark book *The New Industrial State* may be nearly sixty years old, but its lessons speak volumes about today. He (almost alone) foresaw that technology would allow the global elite to aggregate both wealth and power. Interacting with him was always rewarding, and he was very good to me. We had dozens of substantive conversations about technology and its impact on society, which is what motivated me to develop my course on computers and society. I did a few lectures when he had to be absent from his course, but my major role was getting the papers graded, which meant hiring a team of fellow graduate students, mainly friends of mine. I got invited to many events at his home and yearly to his summer home in Vermont. That is how I learned that the rich and the powerful are just humans.

One day, he got a call from a friend who wanted a recommendation for a young economist to write an eclectic monthly newsletter on the economy for his clients. Galbraith recommended me, and I got a quick initiation into a world I did not know existed. His friend was Yura Arkus Duntov who was the CEO of the brokerage subsidiary of Equity Funding, Inc., which was then a Wall Street darling. His brother, Zora Arkus Duntov, is better known for developing the Chevrolet Corvette. Anyway, I took the assignment with my friend and classmate, Dick Rippe, and we met monthly with Yura—time I will always treasure.

The one strange thing I noticed immediately was the questions I got about my request for expense reimbursement. "Surely you spent more? You did not go see a play while you were in New York?" That should have been a clue. Anyway, this assignment went down in flames when the parent company was shown to be a fraud in 1973. The broker-age subsidiary was clean, but that did not matter in the end. Equity Funding offered whole life policies. A whole life policy is a hybrid investment combining life insurance with an investment that gets to accumulate tax free. Equity Funding was very successful at marketing and had remarkable returns for its shareholders. However, as happens, one quarter it was going to miss its numbers. Management realized that there was a way to falsify the numbers to maintain the growth. The industry operated on trust, and an insurer could sell a policy for cash for a multiple of its annual premium to a reinsurer because nearly all policies were renewed year after year. Thus, Equity Funding could create phony policies and show growth because reinsurers would buy those phony policies.

This is not simple, so they purchased a Data General mini-computer and installed it next to the CEO's office. Henceforth, the real books of the company ran there and not on the IBM mainframe.

Data General NOVA 2 microcomputer (1973)

The output from the printers on the mainframe at the time was 144 characters wide, so they cleverly did not have room for all of the policy number. This allowed them to pro-duce an actual folder for each account. The only challenge came at year's end when they had to align the systems. To do this, they transferred the information technology staff from

Los Angeles to New Jersey before Christmas and then back in early January. Reports were that they had over 60,000 phony policies when they went bankrupt in April 1973.

One quarter became many quarters, so they had to scale the production of the phony policies. To do this, they divided the applications into four blocks, which meant that from four real policies you could create twelve additional phony policies. This task went to Department Y. To staff Department Y, they held a rally on Fridays to hire secretaries and had applicants take an aptitude test. This is fifty years ago, so forgive me for the sexism, but the applicants were all women. A cheerleader would tell them to do their best and that every Friday women who had been turned down everywhere else often got a job at Equity Funding.

If an applicant scored 90 or better, she was interviewed to be a secretary. If she scored 40 to 60, she was interviewed for Department Y. They needed people who could be trained to do the cut-and-paste that was required but who were unlikely to see how illegal it was. There are stories of some figuring it out, but saving their jobs was more important.

Management then figured out that they had a new problem. They had sold so many phony policies that some of the policy holders had to die, or the reinsurers would get suspicious. The solution was "charades-like" parties where couples would draw names from a hat and then make up a phony death certificate. There were prizes for the most imaginative. Reading about this is where I learned that at that time about a dozen people a year died from beach umbrellas; that mode of death did not win the most imaginative. Anyway, the policy payoffs improved cash flow.

This was very systematic fraud. Imaginative. Eventually, a financial analyst, Raymond Dirks, exposed the fraud in his newsletter and then went public. He was charged with insider trading by the SEC and had to go to the US Supreme Court to win acquittal. The top executives and three auditors either pleaded or were found guilty of various crimes. As with every consulting job I ever had, I learned a lot. Yura was a great teacher of how his industry worked, and studying the fraud was certainly informative. In particular, the role of the auditors was problematic. Eventually, they went to jail. The idea that people can be long-term business partners and still maintain objectivity enough to blow the whistle just collides with human nature.

Thus, Galbraith educated me in the world in so many other ways. I learned anew that people are people. Dinners at his home were a delight. How else did a twentysomething have dinner with Julia Child, the king and queen of Bhutan, senators, or Gloria Steinem? An unforgettable memory is the Saturday after the 1972 election when I was privileged to attend a dinner party of eight, including Senator George McGovern, who had just lost the presidential election to Richard Nixon.

Galbraith was always gracious and never made a big deal out of status. One night at his home in Vermont I was introduced to the other couple and their son who had joined us. The husband, Bob, and I got into an extended conversation on American literature. I was horrified when I heard Galbraith say as they left, "Great to see you, Penn. We need to do this again soon." I had been arguing with Robert Penn Warren, perhaps the greatest living writer of American literature at the time.

My first trip to London was memorable as well because of Galbraith. Dinner with Sir Roy Harrod and a weekend with Sir Roy Jenkins, then the chancellor of the exchequer, although that had to cancel—though I got an exceptional tour of the Palace of Westminster.

Individually, any of these acts may seem inconsequential, but in total they have had a massive impact on my life. Another professor of mine, Thomas Schelling, wrote about this in "On the Ecology of Micromotives." He was known for his out-of-the-box thinking and is widely credited with creating the Cold War strategy of mutually assured destruction. He was thought to be the model for Dr. Strangelove in the movie of the same name. I lost touch with him until one day ten years ago when he fainted on me on a flight from Copenhagen and smashed my MacBook Air.

Schelling emphasized the importance of costless gestures. Things that one person can do for another that are costless to the giver but valuable, even invaluable, to the receiver. Letting another driver into your lane, for example. This is the very definition of being a mentor: explaining to another not only what to do but why and how, when you have no obligation to do so. Costless gestures are incredibly important.

As I wrote above, Hollis Chenery was also gracious with those gestures. Why did he explain that I needed to learn to read upside down and backwards so that I could read everything on his desk when we met? This was my introduction to the concept of leaking. Or the sentence that if present at the end of a letter to a dean meant, "Ignore the above and reject this request."

A succession of mentors guided me through this decade.

Hank Berry, the neighbor who got me the job at the mineral research institute and was eventually disappointed when I left chemistry for economics. Ken Alexander, who ignited my love for economics. Walter Adams at Michigan State, who made my graduation possible by caring about a confused and crushed young man rebuffed by a departmental assistant. At Harvard, Marc Nerlove, George Eads, Hollis Chenery, Henry Rosovsky, Ken Arrow, Arthur Smithies, and of course Galbraith, were also all incredibly supportive.

CHAPTER 3

THE INSTITUTE FOR DEFENSE ANALYSES (1977–1978)

A FTER WORLD WAR II, THE AIR FORCE CREATED THE RAND COR-PORATION, a think tank devoted to research and development. The Army and the Navy soon created their own. Legally these were FCRCs, Federal Contract Research Centers. The secretary of defense and the joint chiefs of staff wanted their own dedicated team, so the Institute for Defense Analyses (IDA) was created in cooperation with five and then twelve major universities. The idea was to attract talent to critical problems—talent that was difficult to attract in a civil service or military role. You were a quasi–civil servant with slightly more pay and fewer rules.

George Eads recommended me for a summer internship there in 1968, and I spent the summer living in an apartment in Alexandria. My next door neighbor was no liberal; he had trained in police work under Mussolini in Italy and was then working as the chief investigator for the Senate Internal Security Subcommittee. His prior job had been with the anti-Communist unit of the Miami-Dade County Sheriff's Department. He was lonely, as his family was still in Miami, so most weeknights we would have a gin and tonic on his balcony. He took me to lunch in the Senate, and I got to meet Barry Goldwater, James Eastland, and Strom Thurmond. As I said, he was not a liberal.

The work at IDA is done in divisions, and I worked in the Program Analysis Division, then run by Bill Niskanen, the namesake of the Niskanen Center. He left that summer, so I got to attend his farewell dinner. He was succeeded by Harry Williams. PAD was as close to economics as I could get, and overall it was just a great place to work: great people and a relaxed atmosphere with serious, challenging work. It was a top-secret-secure facility. The computer room had copper-covered walls to prevent leakage.

They had two human resource practices that helped maintain quality. When a director left a division, his last act was to lay off all the people he perceived to be deadwood. You found the notice when you came to work the next day. When you went to the new director, he feigned surprise but demurred to his predecessor. Not written down, I am sure, but very effective.

The other practice was a human being, Tom Shirhall. He was the assistant director of human resources and chief recruiter. IDA preferred great talent even for short periods of time over lesser talent for longer periods. IDA had a large stable of consultants. Tom mined those to find people in transition and recruit them. It worked for me.

So, in the middle of a January snowstorm, I moved from Cambridge to Arlington, Virginia. I was afraid the snowstorm would prevent the move, because there was no way the moving van could get into the parking lot to load. A phone call to the local police told me it was impossible to close the street to load, but then I offered to pay for a police detail in case there were any issues. Amazingly, a vote of the city council was no longer required, and forty-five minutes later my street was closed.

My first in-depth lesson about how Washington really works came over aircraft carriers. I was on an IDA team building a complex nonlinear simulation model for naval combat. It was, especially for the time, an incredible intellectual achievement. Feed in the parameters of the war you needed to fight, and the model gave you the optimal force structure to fight that war. In particular, the model forecast how many carrier groups the Navy required. Everyone on the team was proud of the work we had done.

The client said it was great, but they asked for a complete and exact copy of the model, including the computer on which it ran as well as all the software and data. We said there was no need, and they said they were the customer. We delivered it to them. We were not exactly sure why, but they were the customer.

Each year as part of the budget process, each military service submitted their estimate of the wars they were prepared to fight as support for their budget request. This estimate was the input to our model. It was mind-numbing detail. I have been building simulation models for decades, and I am not sure why, but most real-world models end up being incredibly sensitive to some seemingly minor inputs.

Popular media called this the butterfly effect: the idea that a butterfly flapping its wings in China would eventually affect the weather in New York. A mathematician might refer to it as a nearly singular Jacobian. Same thing. Small changes to some inputs can yield large changes to model outputs.

When I was a graduate student, there was a story of a professor at MIT who tragically lost the magnetic tape containing his data. All was not lost, however, as he had the data backed up on punch cards. Yes, people really did that. However, when he reran his weather model with the data from the cards, all the results were different. Enormous effort was applied to find the source of the error, but none was found because there was none. The magnetic tapes stored the data to an accuracy of 7.1 decimal digits—the punch cards to 7.

Our client used this reality in reverse to their advantage. They fiddled with the inputs until they found the least obvious, most minor changes which guaranteed that the model would generate a need for fourteen carrier groups. They then modified the force posture statement and gave it to us to run, and computers being computers, we got the same answer. They then summoned our leader to a classified briefing in Congress where he testified correctly that given that force posture statement, the model of which he was so proud said that fourteen carrier groups were required. He was a distinguished and respected researcher, and his testimony was impactful. The fourteen carrier groups were approved.

In 1978 I was assigned to a task force to study airport security. Because they had the only federal law enforcement presence at airports, preventing hijacking went to the Bureau of Customs at the Treasury Department, and we worked with a wonderful, dedicated deputy assistant secretary. For those who do not know, the deputy assistant secretaries are the people in the federal government who actually get things done or not. President Clinton realized this and met with them, but most presidents ignore them even though half are political appointees.

This was very early in the history of passenger screening, so we started with a clean sheet of paper. We quickly realized that screening items was inefficient and ineffective. Something that Israel figured out also. The thing to screen was people, but doing this meant making judgments. We suggested measuring the amount of adrenalin in the passenger, which is doable from body odors. The electronics in 1978 were fairly primitive, but we made a device that worked reasonably well except that it could not distinguish between adrenalin and having recently consumed jalapeño peppers. The results appeared as racial targeting, so it was a fail.

Our team leader was determined that this was the best way, however, and found an alternative. He trained gerbils to respond to human adrenalin and created a podium with a fan blowing the body odors to a tray underneath the top of the podium. When the gerbils in the tray smelled the adrenalin, they began to move rapidly, signaling the agent to do further inspection. However, when we explained this to the deputy assistant secretary, he ended the effort, as he could not see explaining this as probable cause to a federal judge. Nevertheless, the basic point was still correct. Screen the people, not their items.

I did other projects that seem minor except to the people affected. The Department of Defense was paying for nearly

40,000 people who worked somewhere in the civilian side of the federal government. The Department of Defense wanted to know where. We tried, but the only path seemed to be sending them all a letter and asking them to tell us by return mail where they worked. If this were a few hundred people, I can maybe understand it, but this was nearly 40,000. No surprise that the Pentagon has failed in all attempts to modernize its payroll system. It was still paying Civil War pensions a few years ago.

The big project we undertook was another lesson in software. One source of persistent inflation was the shortage of skilled tradesmen. This was not a national shortage but a series of local shortages. The Labor Department wanted to address this by forecasting by market the demand for construction labor. To do this, they were going to use the F. W. Dodge reports, which track construction activity across the country. (I would encounter them again later at McGraw-Hill.)

The team had constructed a standard input-output matrix, which converted the Dodge activity reports into an estimated need for labor by type. As was typical for the government, the development of the software went to a separate contractor, who wrote software in Cobol to implement the model. To be fair to them, they were not economists and had no idea matrix algebra existed. Unfortunately for the project, while the software worked, each run cost $83,000, which made the effort infeasible. I complained that this was far too high given the work that had to be done.

On a Friday, this confrontation came to a head, and the deputy assistant secretary in charge said enough was enough. He ordered the firm to give me the data and gave me until Monday to do better. It really was trivial, because I understood matrix algebra and knew the formulas they were implementing cell by cell in Cobol. It was not a lot of code, but I got the same answers for $83. To save their honor, the firm rewrote my program in Cobol to lower the cost to $64, but the DAS did not care about that. Design swamps implementation.

I enjoyed the people and enjoyed the work, but I had to move on in true IDA fashion. Joe Kasputys called, and I started talking to Data Resources.

CHAPTER 4

DATA RESOURCES, INC. (1978–1983)

OHN F. KENNEDY DID SOMETHING RARE AS PRESIDENT: HE MADE ECONOMICS RESPECTABLE. The change in attitude was incredible to watch. Economists played a major role in his administration. James Tobin from Yale, who became the chairman of the Council of Economic Advisers, devised the most successful fiscal policy measure of all time, the Investment Tax Credit. John Kenneth Galbraith became the ambassador to India. The profession was on a high. One of my graduate school classmates summarized it simply: "Economists are just a higher form of life."

Economic models were just becoming feasible, and people talked about running the economy as if it were a machine. Models were developed for everything. Development economics, where I was specializing, became almost nothing but models. Companies hired economists and gave them major roles, something that would not happen again for over a half century. Being an economist was cool.

Eventually, the wisdom of John Tukey, one of the greatest statisticians of all time, prevailed: far better a vague answer to the right question than a precise answer to the wrong question, because you can formulate the wrong question in such a way as to permit as precise an answer as you wish. If you read the history of the Vietnam War and the role of Robert McNamara and his use of data, you will understand the gravity of this observation. This was the basic premise of my PhD dissertation.

In this setting, Otto Eckstein, a professor of economics at Harvard, joined with Donald Marron, the president of Mitchell Hutchins, then a prominent investment bank. While we never saw Don Marron, one of my colleagues noted later that whenever a critical decision had to be made by Otto, he would ask for time to think about it. He would then retreat into his office, and observant eyes would see a phone line activated. When the call finished, Otto would tell us his decision.

Otto gave Mitchell Hutchins economic advice, and together he and Don Marron launched Data Resources, Inc. in 1969 to sell the same economic modeling as a service. Chris Snyder, whom I met at DRI, where he ran the New York office, told me that Otto was taken on road trips by Don Marron and hated them. He said he wanted to be replaced by a computer. Otto forged a deal with Burroughs to use their computers to offer this service via timesharing. Technologically, this proved to be a wise decision—Burroughs systems were much better at timesharing than were its competitors'. IBM computers were designed around batch processing, not interactive use.

Timesharing meant users sat at a remote terminal connected to the mainframe computer in Lexington,

Massachusetts, via telephone lines. This was pioneering, and making it work reliably was a feat. DRI opened offices around the country, and each office had its own bank of phone lines.

The vision Otto had was to sell economic models and data to organizations. DRI offered a full menu. Its databank had by far and away the best economic statistics in the world. While the data was legally freely available from the government, it was seldom clean. There were always artifacts, and DRI eliminated those. The data was then readily available in a consistent framework. No one else came close.

Next on the menu was an assortment of models starting with a foundation of the US economy, which was Otto's personal product. It got augmented over time by sector models, each of which was headed by a senior economist. These economists were the princes of DRI, with the swagger (and compensation) to match. Unfortunately, they were not the real business.

Third on the menu was the ability to create and operate your own models. Often these were slight modifications to the DRI model, but this allowed the customers to claim the value of the forecasts as their own . . . and to blame DRI if it proved wrong. A winning formula.

This was the theory. The reality was very different. Don McLagan was hired to run the field organization, and he and his team of regional vice presidents were the people who made DRI what it became. The regional vice presidents all ran slightly different business models and molded the business to their personalities, but the foundation of the business was service consulting.

Don was underappreciated. His wisdom still informs my life. (The day he was promoted to executive vice president,

I met him coming down the stairs in the Lexington office. I congratulated him and wished him a good day. He said he was going to try; after all, he said, you are lucky to get even ten days a year when you can be unambiguously happy. I have learned how right he was.) Don was always customer focused. If someone asked him to review something, he would graciously take it, immediately put it into his briefcase (yes, we carried briefcases then), and assure the person he would get to it as soon as he could. He did not lie—but his office was piled with dozens of briefcases filled with papers waiting to be reviewed.

Don instituted a model of service consulting in which support was free. Well, usage was billed, so not free, but appearances mattered. Service consultants were typically bright, energetic new college graduates who came for two years before leaving for business school. Customers loved having them around. And they were peers to the analysts typically doing the work. Social relationships between them and the customers were not uncommon. Don later figured out that these consultants became more profitable to the company over time, so he instituted a program with large bonuses for staying a third year. Another year of growth ensued.

Otto was convinced that models and information were the foundation of the business, and he insisted that customers be charged for the usage of the data (a change I instituted much later when I became the pricing officer). The underlying economics conundrum was this: Computers at the time were very expensive. They required a dedicated, expensive facility and lots of staff. However, those costs were fixed. On the margin, the cost of computing was zero, but the average cost was not. Everyone used algorithms of some sort to charge people for use. The customers paid real dollars as a result, but internal users paid nothing—though they were far and away the largest users. Once internal charges were considered, all the economic models were money losers except for Otto's, which almost everyone bought.

When Otto was presented with paperwork showing that all the models lost money except for his, and that data usage was minimal, he threw the printout into the air and said, "This is not a company I want to run." He resigned the next day. The free time he gained allowed him to get a physical examination he had postponed, and, tragically, he died from cancer shortly thereafter.

The real business of DRI was personal computing in a world without personal computers. Otto had assembled a mélange of software at the beginning and then had the good fortune to hire a brilliant programmer, Robert P. Lacey, to write the next generation, the Econometrics Programming System, EPS. I doubt I will ever encounter a more brilliant piece of software, decades ahead of its time. We added both APL and Speakeasy as options, but neither gained serious market share (although APL gained some because its internal owner convinced the company to use a different pricing algorithm, which effectively discounted it heavily).

By 1976, I had written all the economics statistical software used at Harvard at the time, but Otto had chosen TSP, the Time Series Processor, from MIT, written by Robert Hall, now a professor at Stanford. Nevertheless, the possibility for me to join DRI was obvious. However, I was an assistant professor at Harvard, and Otto was a full professor.

More importantly, Bob Lacey was the chief architect, so any role for me was going to be limited. I did not fit any boxes.

However, I started doing some part-time consulting for John Lauer, who was the vice president of operations. John was the first of the several operations executives I met in my career, undervalued and underpaid. John made the trains run on time, which was a really hard job then. It took very different skills, including vendor management and attention to detail, and as a result he was a fish out of water on the management team.

John asked me to create a benchmark we could use to put in the contracts with Burroughs so that we could pay them on the actual amount of work their computers could deliver. It was a fun assignment, and I learned a lot about how Burroughs computers worked (which was totally different from every other computer on the market). He wanted to hire me full-time, and we discussed possible roles.

At the time, I was coming up for promotion to associate professor at Harvard. I never really expected it, as usually only one in eight was promoted at that time. That may have been a mistake on my part. All the statistical research at Harvard was done on my software, and some of its capabilities were unique. It allowed research in ways and on large datasets that was simply not possible anywhere else. As I've mentioned, at least one professor earned a Nobel Prize because of that research.

One day, I got a phone call from James Duesenberry, the chairman of the Department of Economics. He told me that the department had discussed the intellectual value of software and had concluded there was none. He said that I was like a glassblower to a chemist. Needless to say, after that call I had no expectations of promotion.

The chairman of the committee to recommend whether I should be promoted was Otto Eckstein. I am not sure whether he had any idea I was talking to DRI. Nevertheless, although I had some prominent champions, I was not promoted. John Kenneth Galbraith asked me what I was going to do, and one option I mentioned was DRI. That set off a flurry of activity I only recently discovered through a web post that resulted in Otto agreeing to cut his Harvard pay in half. And a few years later I went off to join the Institute for Defense Analyses.

Joe Kasputys was hired as the vice president running DRI's Washington office. Joe knew where the business really was. In 1978, he hired me as a technical manager and installed me in an office next to him. It was never clear what my role was, really. I was just there. I was not that well paid and received no equity.

My first major assignment was the Multiple Award Schedule Contract (MASC) with the General Services Administration. This would make it markedly easier for government customers to buy DRI services. There is an old saying in Washington, "In any negotiation with the government there are two sides: one which gives a lot, and the government." This was no different. At the end of every negotiation, you must agree to a clause that says the government can cancel at any time if it wants to without compensation. It is the law.

The challenge for DRI was that the government insisted upon most-favored-nation pricing: the government always got the lowest commercial price regardless of terms. There is a loophole—alternate pricing schemes are allowed if there are realistic circumstances in which the scheme would yield higher prices. The human challenge is that these contracts are negotiated with contracting officers, who are dedicated civil servants with sometimes very limited knowledge of the reality of the services being priced.

Anyway, we got it, and revenues grew. I then got involved in a study on revenue sharing. For a while, the federal government shared revenue with the states on a statistical basis, and I helped with the data analysis. This made me familiar with county-level data. This is vastly more complicated than it seems, because the definition of a county varies across states.

DRI then got a contract from the Department of Commerce (really for the White House) to analyze the Economic Development Act of 1965. This act provided federal government grants to local communities to boost economic development, but the criteria for approval were very loose. Members of Congress loved the act, mostly the local press releases trumpeting their efforts to bring federal dollars home.

To get the grants, a county had to be distressed according to a formula. However, the law was once distressed, always distressed. There was no mechanism for a county to become undistressed once it was so designated. As a result, roughly 97 percent of the country was legally distressed by 1979.

The Carter administration wanted to reform this. Eventually, they struck a deal with Norman Mineta, the chair of the relevant subcommittee in the House. I was told he agreed to a reform on two conditions: 90 percent of the country had to remain distressed, and that 90 percent had to include all the counties in his congressional district. My assignment was to find a formula that did that and could pass a smell test.

I did so on Sunday, September 30, 1979. The deadline was the next day. DRI computing was very expensive, and it took a lot of data mining. It cost a million dollars in computer time. No one complained; for the time, the bill was reasonable. Key to the formula was excessive employment growth, which allowed the counties near San Jose, California, to qualify.

Unknown to me, DRI was in talks to sell itself to McGraw-Hill, Inc. but was going to miss its financial goals for the quarter. I changed that with the million-dollar bill. The company sold for a record $103 million, and the sale made lots of people lots of money, though not me. I did get a thank-you phone call from the CFO.

McGraw-Hill had a policy that every operating company had to have an executive vice president in place so the CEO could be fired at any time. DRI needed such a person, and as the head of the most successful region in the company (in part because of the million-dollar bill), Joe Kasputys assumed that role and promoted me to run software.

The software team that developed and maintained EPS was, shall we say, autonomous. They made their own decisions, and they ran the syntax committee, which determined product direction. Management was an abstract and irrelevant construct to them. I was definitely an alien. I soon realized that direction was impossible; they had to be courted and influenced.

I mastered the art of leaving work at 6, shopping by 6:30, and having dinner ready by 7. I hosted dinners for the team in whole or in part at least once a week. We developed a reasonable working relationship. One developer, Peter White, probably wrote 60,000 or more lines of Algol per year. (Algol was the assembly language for Burroughs.) By way of comparison, the average at IBM at that time was a little over 100 for lines of code put into production per year. Peter was a loner and not a dinner guest.

One feature I really wanted was dynamic linking. I had used a similar feature heavily when I wrote in PL-1 for the IBM mainframe at Harvard. It was my "secret sauce." You could exit to assembly language for certain tasks, which let you do some magical things that were otherwise impossible. I wanted a similar feature in EPS to exit to an Algol program.

For over a year I was stalled on this. I was given estimates of years of effort and expense to add it. One Saturday night I was working late and took Jon Osser out to pizza. Jon was a great musician and a brilliant developer. He really did not need to work because he was the voice in the Campbell's soup commercials and got monthly royalty checks. I had to beg him to cash his payroll checks.

At dinner I explained why I thought dynamic linking was so important. We returned to work. An hour later he demonstrated it to me. The previous work estimates were obviously incorrect. Dynamic linking essentially unlocked a wealth of new revenue opportunities because anyone could extend EPS with very little effort. That was probably my only real contribution to the language, though Otto and I did write and publish an explanation of EPS and why it mattered.

Like most of the great executives I encountered in my career, Don McLagan was a leader much more than a manager. Success came from hiring and recruitment, not detailed plans and reviews. His staff were evaluated not on paper but on customer results and meetings. He was not naïve about the hazards of corporate life. More than once he reminded me that there was only one signature on the corporate contract, and that was yours. If you wanted to play the corporate game, prepare to lose now and then. It went with the territory.

I came to understand this last lesson better shortly after he said it to me. I had lunch with a colleague who was seen as the superstar of the company. He was a great person in most respects, but he was someone who thought that his compensation plan was a "license to kill" as long as an action helped his compensation metrics. One day he badly berated a junior employee in a meeting. I asked him why, as it had served no purpose. He answered simply, "When I see someone bent over, I fuck them on principle." Not very collegial. I met many like that over the years.

Don's best advice came the day I was promoted to vice president. I was happy. Better title, better office, more money, and more opportunity. Don brought back reality by asking, "What did you lose?" His answer was that I had lost the right not to err. And that was big. (I also was looking forward to having a couch in my office, a privilege of the title. Alas, that day Otto ordered all couches removed from the offices, because of inappropriate behavior discovered the night before.)

At the urging of my boss and others, I looked to hire a manager for EPS. One of our customers seemed well suited. He had great knowledge of its actual use and seemingly solid business sense. After exhaustive interviews and support from colleagues, I made an offer, which he accepted. His first day did not go well. After meeting with the team, they all came to me and said they were resigning if he stayed. I terminated him that day, but the company found him another role. He was clearly the best of the candidates, but he was not good enough.

My real job was to grow the revenues of our ten largest clients, as measured at year end. I did well at this, though the design of the metric favored me. The fastest-growing accounts always made the top 10 list. In talking to these customers, I realized that our biggest failings were not features but support. And I did talk to them, becoming a frequent flyer.

I created a two-person technical consulting group to help our service consultants. Jim Savage and Dennis Cunningham became invaluable instantly and were a constant source of product ideas. I had to find ways to give them time off the phones so they would not leave. I asked a former English teacher to write a manual, knowing she was not technical. She did a great job.

By now personal computers were on the radar. The state of the art was an Apple II, and it was a long way from EPS. But maybe our customers did not need all the power of EPS. Maybe a spreadsheet was enough. Customers clearly did not like their monthly charges. I ended up championing three projects: VAX, DRILink, and DataKits.

EPS was a big, complicated set of software. Customers wanted it to run in-house on a capital budget, not an operating budget. The team evaluated our options and selected VAX from Digital Equipment Corporation (DEC) as the platform. We started off with great hopes, but the reality was that porting EPS was always doomed to failure. Algol on Burroughs was wonderful for certain things, and EPS was one of those. After I left, they attempted to port to IBM, but that was even harder. Time ran out.

DRILink was the best of what was feasible at the time. The goal was to provide a much cheaper option running on UNIX-based, microcomputer-based systems in the customer's office. These were all the rage around 1980, with many vendors competing for share. We built a solid team and delivered a decent software stack, eventually going back to Bob Lacey to write a language. But the clock ran out again. PCs were getting better faster.

DRILink was a great business success, however, even if it was a failure as a product. It showed innovation. It was a reason to call on customers. Most importantly, it kept the customers spending money on EPS while they waited. I suspect Joe Kasputys wanted DRILink to exist but not succeed. If so, he was brilliant.

One side note. We hired a contractor to write a spreadsheet for DRILink. It was good, but we never got volume. He used that experience and code to write another spreadsheet that did better for another company: Lotus 1-2-3. That is why Lotus 1-2-3 seemed somewhat like EPS, because we asked for that compatibility.

The last major effort I championed was DataKits, which we did in partnership with VisiCorp. This was a truly path-breaking product. The late Bill Coleman, who later went on to run software at Sun, start BEA Systems, and then bring Veritas back, was my partner in crime. The contract was negotiated with Dan Fylstra, the co-founder of VisiCorp.

My only background on Dan came from my graduate school classmate, the late Charlie Kelso. Charlie was Dan's professor at Harvard Business School, and he was asked for advice on Dan's idea for this startup to commercialize the idea of a spreadsheet, which Dan Bricklin had invented. Charlie advised Dan that it had no future. Fortunately for Dan, he ignored Charlie's advice.

We went through days of friendly but tough negotiation. After all, this was all new. There were no precedents. I was alone in California on a Friday after 5 p.m. Eastern time, so the corporate office in New York was closed. Dan made an ultimatum, and I left. As I was about to start my car to leave, someone came out to ask me to return, and we signed shortly thereafter.

Bill's team created Apple II software called VisiLink, which connected to DRI over a dial-up modem. At DRI, a VisiLink session looked like an EPS user and invoked a special EPS workspace. You filled out a form saying what data you wanted. A bill was created. You paid by credit card. EPS created a spreadsheet with the data, which was downloaded to your Apple II. You could then access the data in VisiCalc, the most popular spreadsheet of the day. The demonstration was awesome. Remember that the internet was still ten years in the future. Later, when Microsoft was sued over some internet patents, I sent the software to Steve Ballmer, because we had prior art for all the patents covered. Unfortunately for them, the Microsoft attorneys did not use it.

McGraw-Hill loved the product and ran a full-page ad in the *Wall Street Journal* the day of its annual shareholders meeting. Over 25,000 inquiries were received. We sold three DataKits, maybe fewer. Turns out no one really wanted the data. VisiCorp went on to chase Microsoft Windows with a graphical user interface and lost interest (and lost that battle). McGraw-Hill was not prepared to invest in advertising. It did get me promoted, but that is another story.

There is one last thread worth covering: the file machine. DRI had lots of data for its time. Computers could not share data, however, so as DRI expanded to multiple computers, data had to be maintained on multiple systems. This was both expensive and cumbersome. A team of DRI engineers came up with a brilliant solution. These engineers wanted to create a file machine. Put all the data onto a minicomputer and then have it imitate a disk drive to the Burroughs mainframes. There is nothing wrong with this idea other than it is hard to implement and we did not own the operating system on the mainframes. It would be a very fun project, even if it failed—which it did. The project lead was smart, but his team was not as strong. Application companies do poorly at building system-level software. I would see this again and again.

The team sold management on it. It looked like the perfect foundation for a future world of the electronic distribution of information over timesharing. I argued strenuously against it not because it was a bad idea but because it was a good idea that would soon be commercially available. That position made me enemies, and I soon lost control of EPS. I was right though.

A startup came calling in 1979 with a software solution for us. I met with the founder and eventually visited their single-office company in Silicon Valley. He was very passionate, but the technology was not a fit for us. It was for others, however. That company was Oracle and the founder was Larry Ellison.

Years later, I realize that we were far more innovative than we realized. We were in a green field solving problems sequentially. We thought we were in a niche business and invested accordingly, but the power of our solutions was far greater. Being on Burroughs systems allowed us to do what we did but eventually ensured our demise as they failed to survive as a computer vendor.

Buried in the operating system was a procedure called OldWeirdHarold. It originally had a different name, but was renamed when its namesake, Harold, retired. Apparently, Harold was a genius, and when other developers would bring him a problem, he would answer with instructions to call this procedure in a specific way. No one else really knew what it did or how it did it. Without it, the system would not work. OldWeirdHarold and EPS taught me again the enormous value a single developer can generate, a lesson that sticks with me today.

CHAPTER 5

MCGRAW-HILL (1983–1985)

MCGRAW-HILL HAD A LONG TRADITION OF A CONSIGLIERI, PEOPLE WITHOUT ANY POWER BUT WITH ENORMOUS INFLUENCE. The title was senior vice president and executive assistant to the CEO. The office was next to the CEO. No one could come or go without being seen by him, as he never closed his door. He was always seemingly on your side, but he was always on the side of the CEO. He was at every meeting that mattered.

In early 1983, the incumbent consiglieri was Tom Sullivan. Tom invited me to come to corporate headquarters to meet with Joe Dionne, the new CEO. I was honored and a bit excited, so I went. McGraw-Hill was already a longstanding company with a lot of formality. The forty-ninth floor was home to the top management and was marked by distinctive blue carpeting. Senior management always got nonstop elevators going down (though not going up—that would be too obvious to the rank and file). There were changing rooms on the forty-ninth floor stocked with underwear, socks, shirts, and the like in case you unexpectedly had to stay the night. Technically, bedrooms were not allowed by law; hence, they were "changing rooms."

Tuesday night was a big night. Most executives had long commutes and left promptly around 5:00 to catch their trains, but on Tuesday nights, almost everyone stayed and worked until late. Unless you were completely dumb, you realized that careers were made and lost on Tuesday night. Both the chairman, Harold McGraw, and the CEO, Joe Dionne, were there, and it was a rare opportunity for a non-transactional conversation.

This was all new to me. Joe was embarking on the major transformation of McGraw-Hill into the leader in digital information. Acquiring Data Resources, Inc. was the first major step in that, but Joe had much bigger ambitions. Remember, the internet would not be invented until ten years later. This was early. Joe knew his CEOs were reluctant, so he planted eight "Young Turks" into the corporation. I was to be the one at corporate. He wanted me to be the burr under the saddle for his CEOs, he said. My job was to be vice president of product development support, which was conceived as being a "product fairy godmother."

"Product fairy godmother" did not really excite me, and I said so to Tom Sullivan, who debriefed me. I was uncertain if I would accept. Tom then explained to me that in McGraw-Hill you only got one invitation to the Blue Carpet, and if you did not accept it, you were soon gone. After this "clarification," I accepted. The Young Turks all became good friends. We would all be gone within three years.

I soon had an office and a small team of great people I knew could integrate into projects and help them along. At McGraw-Hill, if you wanted to start something that was going to lose money, you needed to assemble a sponsor group. Members had to be senior executives not in your management chain, and each quarter they had to commit in writing to support your money-losing project. If you already were a business and missed your numbers two quarters in a row, you went on the fix-fold-or-sell list run by the consiglieri. You then fixed the business, closed it, or sold it. This was certain.

Apparently, I was doing a good job, and soon I was promoted to senior vice president and chief scientist. An odd title for a media company. An odd title in any event. I was the youngest person ever made a corporate senior vice president. My job did not really change, but as a senior vice president I attended more meetings that mattered, including meetings of the board of directors.

I did not really have a job. There was nothing that required my signature. But I had a lot of influence. One reason was that most Tuesday evenings I would get summoned to the CEO's office, and we would talk for one to two hours. He would tell me not only what was going on in the company, but also why. He kept seventy-five personnel folders in his desk drawer. These were the seventy-five people he thought made the company run (out of over 14,000 employees). Another important lesson.

At the first board meeting I attended, Joe began by saying he wanted to build the plan for the next fiscal year to achieve a 15 percent growth in earnings per share. This was a surprise to the staff, who knew this was a nearly impossible goal. Harold McGraw interrupted him immediately to say how pleased he was with that goal. Harold had turned down an acquisition offer and needed to prove that doing so was the correct decision.

At the next meeting, Joe began by saying that 15 percent was the goal, but achieving it would take perfect execution. To assure that, he was promoting Don Fruehling, the president of the McGraw-Hill Book Company, to executive vice president of operations (COO). He said, probably correctly, that Don was the best operator in the company. I went in later that night to congratulate Don, and he thanked me. He then said that he had actually been fired. There was no way to make the numbers, and Joe knew it. He assured me that two board meetings hence, Joe would begin with, "You never know the mark of a man until you put him in the role. Don could not operate at the corporate level and left the company this morning. We will miss the numbers." He was right almost to the word.

I later learned that there was a lot of Kabuki theater at McGraw-Hill, like at most institutions. Harold McGraw had lost his enthusiasm for Joe, who was a PhD, to whom he had just given a ten-year contract. Don was his candidate to replace him. Joe dodged a bullet and eliminated a contender all at once. Well played.

I spent a lot of time and energy on acquisitions. My first was an Arizona company that had the best accounting software running on Windows PCs. It was remarkably good. Input your chart of accounts, and it did the rest. Only problem? The customer base generally had no idea what its chart of accounts was, and it lost in the marketplace to much worse software that was tailored to particular markets. Think veterinarians or Baptist churches.

Joe named a task force to identify the future source of competitive advantage. This had most of his eight plants on it, and we worked well as a group. Out of it came a conclusion valid to this day: customer-specific application knowledge. I learned that a franchise was market power that could be attacked, but only by incurring massive operating losses. McGraw-Hill was a collection of franchises, some of which were incredibly profitable.

The next acquisition I was asked to help on was Borland software in Scotts Valley, California. This was a cultural mismatch that is hard to describe. I went by myself for a due diligence visit, and I dressed more or less California style. When I arrived, the founder, the legendary Philippe Kahn, looked at me and said, "Thank God. Not another fucking suit." He then ripped off his tie, and we had a good conversation including a lunch somewhere with around six women who worked at Borland.

When he had no money at the beginning, Philippe needed advertising, and the place he needed to advertise was in *Byte* magazine, owned by McGraw-Hill. The day the salesperson from *Byte* arrived, he made a phony advertising plan with Ziff-Davis, its competitor, and left it on the whiteboard in his office. Once the meeting started, he made an excuse and left the room. He had drilled a hole in the wall so he could see what was happening. Eventually, the *Byte* salesperson found the Ziff-Davis plan. Philippe then returned, and the salesperson offered him a counter including a large amount of upfront, free advertising. He took it, and the rest was history. And now McGraw-Hill wanted to buy what he had built.

The deal went forward, and a recommendation was made to the board to approve the acquisition. My job was to entertain Philippe the night before, and we had a memorable dinner at the River Café in Brooklyn. The next morning the *Wall Street Journal* ran a story about Borland, including that the company had toga parties and that Philippe was an illegal alien, among other things. The acquisition never came to a vote. Rumor says he leaked the story because he did not want to sell, even though his investors did. I did get to make my first visit to Copenhagen as part of the due diligence.

We bought another company that specialized in long-distance calling rates. They sold databases that companies could use to route their long-distance calls most cheaply. The formula used at McGraw-Hill to value acquisitions was dominated by the terminal value, usually ten times the final year profit. I argued strenuously that this was not a business to buy, because soon long-distance rates would be zero. I was actually laughed at.

Joe was very committed to being the leader in electronic distribution of information, as I mentioned above. He hired Michael Porter, a professor at the Harvard Business School, and his company, the Monitor Group, to drive this journey. I knew Michael slightly from my Harvard days, and the project leader had once been my student. Michael was widely touted as the leader in this field. He coined the phrase *the turbine* as our objective. Remember that the internet would not exist for another ten years.

I set out to deliver the turbine. My search led me to a small company, Monchik-Weber, and its CEO, Leon Williams. Leon patented the concept of publish-and-subscribe information distribution, which meant you broadcast the information widely and each end-point subscribed to the information it wanted. Monchik-Weber created the first system that delivered real-time stock prices to local computers so you could compute things like averages in real-time and trade on them. It created the world of finance we know today, along with ever-more-powerful local computers. Nothing else was close.

My boss, Brent Harries, who was the former CEO of Standard and Poor's, was not a technologist at all, but he saw the potential and pushed for the acquisition, in large part because he wanted to be an operator again and not staff. It was surprisingly easy to get the acquisition approved, but there was a last-minute switch to have it report to Howard Hosbach, the CEO of S&P. When the acquisition later failed, the board hired McKinsey to investigate why, and Howard left the company.

Howard was a good guy, but definitely not one to run emerging technology. One day I was summoned along with several other people to his office. S&P ran the Blue List, which was the listing of municipal bonds available for sale. There were roughly six thousand terminals, and a printed report was delivered each business day. The bonds are in high denomination, and the market is specialized. The information into S&P all arrived on paper and was entered manually and then reviewed before being published.

A woman working in data input opened a bond, for a hospital in California then in the news, and added a comment line to amuse her boyfriend who worked upstream as an editor. I cannot repeat the line here, but it was singularly offensive. At his dismissal hearing, he swore he hit the delete button and not the return key, but it went out to all the terminals instantly and was in the printed register the next morning.

A customer had paid $10,000 for the listing, and Howard felt he needed to call him. He kept saying he should call by noon. We all agreed ... but it was now 11:55 a.m. He finally called, and the customer answered.

"Mr. Hosbach," he said. "I have been expecting your call."

Howard immediately apologized and explained their processes to avoid errors like this. The customer cut him off and suggested the processes should be reviewed. Howard's face told his distress, but the customer ended with, "I have had the bond listed for two weeks with no interest. Sold it at 9:03 a.m. this morning." (The market opened at 9:00.) Then he hung up.

We needed distribution, and that got us to a meeting with John Malone in Denver. John controlled a large cable company and had been working on using similar technology to that used by Monchik-Weber to deliver information. The potential fit was great, but the cultural obstacles were greater. We had a great meeting with John, but the effort just lapsed over time.

The F. W. Dodge reports were another project. The reports were collected on pieces of paper by reporters, mainly housewives who worked part-time. The reports were mailed to New York, and there they were processed and entered into an IBM Series One computer. The software calculated how many times the report would fit onto a mimeograph master. The master was produced with the number of copies to be made and a set of punch cards. The copies were then cut into individual slips using a paper cutter, and the slips and the punch cards were put into a queue.

At 3 p.m., a squad of high school students arrived and put on roller skates. They picked up the stack of slips and the punch cards. The punch cards were coded for racks of pigeonholes, and each card lit up the holes in a given rack to receive that slip. The students skated around the room inserting cards and depositing slips as directed. I am not making this up. It was so cheap. We could not come close to matching the cost electronically.

In general, my time was divided between advising on internal projects and corporate development, generally meaning finding new revenue streams. We attempted to find something with IBM, but mating these two companies was impossible. There was no obvious overlap. Similarly, a conversation between David Kearns, CEO of Xerox, and Joe Dionne led to my being tasked with exploring possible cooperation. Nothing happened in the end, except that Xerox became my next employer.

Roger Levien, the vice president of strategy for Xerox, and I spent many hours trying to identify a possible project. We actually made good progress and defined an Information Appliance as something that could be sold by Xerox and fulfilled by McGraw-Hill. Personal computers were nascent at the time, and the internet did not exist (although networks did). We had just acquired Monchik-Weber as well. As often happens, this was a good idea for an instant in time but could never be developed and sold fast enough to not be obsolete at the time of introduction. In any event, future events meant this project died.

In 1985, McGraw-Hill management went to Absecon, NJ, for an offsite to agree on future strategy. I was the keynote speaker. It was a good speech, but it marked my end as well. Joe Kasputys had been the CEO of Data Resources, and in one of those Kabuki theater moves, he had been taken out of the role and given a consolation prize of executive vice president at corporate. He had one direct report, me. On his first day in the office, he asked me into a conference room where he told me that there was only room for one of us in the company, and he would win. He did.

I went to see Dionne after that first meeting, and Joe said not to worry. Kasputys had a job at the Harvard Business School and was leaving in a few months. I left on a vacation, and the secretaries later told me Kasputys watched me cross the street and then went to tell Dionne that he was staying and that I had to go. Kasputys had been lobbying Harold McGraw, so Dionne did not have a free hand. Dionne did make a very supportive call to David Kearns, the CEO at Xerox, which secured my next role.

In a move that still shocks me, Tom Sullivan, who had been helpful all along, asked me to do a final favor. The company was rolling out the Absecon strategy to the staff and had a large meeting planned. He asked me to present the speech I did at Absecon. I did my duty, but it was not easy. I learned the truth of Don McLagan: the corporate contract only has one signature on it.

CHAPTER 6

XEROX (1985-1988)

N 1985, XEROX WAS AN ICONIC COMPANY, ADMIRED FOR ITS PRO-
FESSIONALISM AND STYLE. Even today its techniques for sales
remain a benchmark. The Xerox 914, the first plain paper
copier, revolutionized the office. Rosemary Fruehling, the
wife of Don Fruehling, my colleague at McGraw-Hill, wrote a
wonderful book on that. You must be as old as I am to appreciate how dramatic was that change.

In 1970 or 1971, I spent a summer as an intern at the
World Bank working for Robert Dorfman, a professor of
mine from Harvard. Our project helped me realize how distant an institution
like Harvard or the
World Bank could be
from the real world.
We were building a
post-war model of
the economy of the
Mekong River Delta.
As a condition of

Xerox 914 (1959)

employment, the Bank had agreed to pay for my apartment. However, since I was not a permanent employee, I had to apply for the allowance. I wrote the appropriate letter and gave it to a secretary to type (yes, that is how the world used to work). She returned it to me with sixteen carbon copies. I asked which copy was for me. The answer was none. The copies all went to different files.

The Bank used IBM electric typewriters, and they had special ones manufactured that were designed for seventeen-part forms, because the regular typewriter could not strike with sufficient force for sixteen carbon copies. And even though the 914 had been around for over a decade, the Bank had yet to adapt its business processes.

This is important for Xerox, because the original marketing consultants they hired sized the total available market for the 914 by the amount of carbon paper sold in the world. Their estimated market size was off by a factor of fifty. The 914 showed the world that the demand for information was virtually infinite. When I reached Xerox, internal research showed that the typical copied document was already a copy of a copy thirteen times!

Xerox competitors never got this. IBM and Kodak copiers were just as good on copy one as Xerox but failed as the generations increased. The key to that was the paper path, and to design it Xerox hired away the brilliant designer of the airframe for the Boeing 747, paying whatever it took.

The misforecast also created a supply problem for Xerox. The copier works by electrically charging a metal drum with toner and then transferring that powder to the paper. After that, the drum must be cleaned. This is much harder than it seems, because the toner is sticky, and the drum cannot be scratched.

Xerox engineers found the perfect solution: the fur of Australian rabbits whom Nature blessed with one stiff hair out of every seven. For a while, the original director of procurement for Xerox worked for me, and he told me the story of calling his supplier, waking him up, to tell him the good news that Xerox needed more rabbit skins. The supplier paused and asked how many and when. The answer was 250,000 in two weeks. The supplier replied that they shot them with a 0.22 caliber rifle, and he thought that fulfilling that order would be hard, since he was sure there were not 250,000 bullets in Australia. Xerox found a synthetic substitute.

What was really innovative for Xerox, however, was the original business model. The legendary CEO Joe Wilson decided not to sell the machines, but rent them at 10 cents per copy. Gold mine. Within offices, control of the Xerox "clicker" was pure power. The beauty was that it just counted pages. No real accountability.

Xerox made its money by selling toner. At one point I calculated that the gross margin at the Oklahoma City toner plant exceeded the total profits of the entire corporation. The risk to Xerox was always that a chemical giant would sell the toner much more cheaply. To avoid this, Xerox made every copier model slightly different so that each needed its own toner, so that it was not economical for a chemical giant to compete. I never saw a stock market analysis that understood this.

Copiers are inherently fragile, so they broke. I once was in a Xerox meeting with the CEO waiting to start, and no one had the courage to tell him that every copier in corporate headquarters was broken. Scale therefore gave Xerox another huge competitive advantage, because they had the biggest service force.

The Japanese ended all this. The US government forced Xerox to license its patents, and the Japanese changed the business model completely. They took the service force back to the factory and made copiers with disposable cartridges containing everything that usually broke. Suddenly the biggest advantage of Xerox became a liability.

Xerox almost died from this, and the only thing that saved them was their 25 percent–owned Japanese affiliate, Fuji Xerox. The entire corporation became fixated on quality. It was not a strategy but a religion. It dominated the culture. When I joined, I was given a special course (indoctrination) before being let into the wild. Xerox came back, and the System 10 saved the company. The name came because the head of marketing saw the Bo Derek movie *10* the night before naming.

As I said above, Xerox was undoubtedly the most professionally managed company in the United States. Process and procedures were honed and followed. A study showed that when the CEO changed the meeting of the leadership team, over 6,000 other calendars had to change, so the CEO stopped changing. Note my choice of words: *professional* is not the same as *best*.

The management team saw that paper would eventually give way to electronics, long before it happened, so they created the Xerox Palo Alto Research Center. PARC proceeded to invent the technology that still dominates the office today: Ethernet, Windows, client server computing, Microsoft Word, graphics,

etc. Their greatest triumphs (though not commercially successful, possibly being ahead of their times) were the Alto and
the Star—which foretold the user interface we use to this day.

Xerox Alto (1973) and Star (1981)

Amazingly, they did all this on computers that were on
the order of 12,000 times less powerful than a modern laptop.
This took brilliant people writing brilliant software. The story
of PARC is amazing and has been better told by others.*

I was assigned to a team that was asked why Xerox made
so little out of the PARC inventions. The bottom-line answer
was probably the Xerox expense account policy. Technology
resides in brains, not paper, and to take the technology from
the proof-of-concept PARC delivered was hard. The brilliant

---

* Hiltzik, Michael A., *Dealers of Lightning: Xerox PARC and the Dawn of the
Computer Age* (New York: HarperCollins, 1999); Smith, Douglas K., Robert
C. Alexander, *Fumbling the Future: How Xerox Invented, Then Ignored, the
First Personal Computer* (New York: William Morrow and Company, 1988);
Waldrop, M. Mitchell, *The Dream Machine: J.C.R. Licklider and the Revo-
lution That Made Computing Personal* (New York: Viking Penguin, 2001).

engineers were not that interested in the nuts and bolts of making the product, so that task went to a different team of engineers who were just not as good. A lot fell through that crack.

The PARC researchers had little incentive to work with internal engineers. If they went to see a Xerox team, they had to fly the cheapest coach fare possible, rent the cheapest rental car, and stay at low-end lodging. Meals were not covered. However, if you were with a third-party wanting to license your technology, they could wine and dine you and provide more comfortable travel. Not surprisingly, the researchers loved those deals.

Thus, while Xerox invented this technology, it never really monetized it. To be fair, software patents were not yet permitted. However, they did create a business to build and sell it, and demonstrations of its power were everywhere. I eventually closed that business. Xerox did have an investment in Apple, however, and as part of that deal Steve Jobs was given a presentation. He got the technology immediately and knew that in the future all computers would work that way.

Jobs went back and asked his engineers a simple question: How much of this can you give me for $2,000? The answer was the Macintosh, created by a team of eight brilliant engineers working in isolation. *This is the power of the question.* Xerox management had asked a similar but totally different question: How much does this cost? The business strategies and outcomes were totally different as a result.

The answer to the Xerox question was about $50,000 a desk, so Xerox invested accordingly. By the time I joined, the product was Viewpoint, and when I got my system, I was amazed. It was so far ahead of anything else. However, given the price, the market was small, and the business was losing money—lots of money.

Here I learned another very important lesson: *your best customers buy your worst products.* One customer was the US Army. At the time, a leading cause of death in the Army was outdated maintenance manuals. They used loose-leaf binders with monthly update sheets. They were never accurately maintained. Xerox technology allowed them to reprint the manuals every month with a different color cover, so it was easy to check that people were using the current manual. Told that Xerox might cancel the workstations, the colonel who was the customer reportedly assured the salesperson that Xerox would never again sell a copier to the Defense Department. There were others. So, Xerox kept losing money.

I was hired by Roger Levien, then vice president of strategy, as a principal in the Corporate Strategy Office. This was a stupid title equivalent to that of a division vice president, but only someone steeped in the arcane world of Xerox would know that. I learned about the thoroughness of Xerox management style through the twenty-six interviews I endured.

Roger oversaw a project called Xerox 95, a strategic planning exercise involving the direct reports to the CEO. Once again, however, this was partly Kabuki theater, as it was really the selection process for the next CEO of Xerox. I am not sure everyone realized that, but Roger's boss sure did. Not surprisingly, he won the race.

Kepner-Tregoe created a framework for strategic planning. They argued that firms could only be one of four paradigms: technology-driven, financially driven, sales-driven, or product driven. The management team was divided into four teams and each given one of the paradigms for which to build a strategic plan. Each team had a principal assigned to do the actual work. I joined and was immediately thrown into the process for the product-driven team.

Of course, as part of the process we regularly briefed the CEO, so we had a pretty good idea of his beliefs and values. I suspect this gave Roger's boss some assistance in navigating the subsequent discussions. We wrote up four cases, and they were all acceptable. There was lots of talent in the company, but in the end the strategy selected was product-driven and focused on document processing. That happened to be my team, and it was a good strategy, though Xerox stayed on it too long. It was meant to be an evolution to electronic focusing on Xerox strengths.

Being thorough again, the principals were sent out to evangelize the strategy. Monthly, I would teach at the Xerox management training center. I was sent one day on a special trip to brief the Southwest regional vice president in Dallas. He was bemused but liked me and took me to a wonderful dinner at Pappa's steakhouse. The dinner was far beyond anything Xerox expense policy allowed, so I offered to pay half. He laughed and said, "Son, when you are 35 percent ahead of plan, there is no expense policy." Another important lesson.

I then asked him how he was so good. I said he was the most successful sales executive in Xerox, which he was. He demurred and offered some platitudes, but I pressed. He then confessed that it was his hiring strategy. I asked what it was. This is not politically correct today, but forty years ago it was. Virtually all the hires were male at the time. He said he tried to figure out whether the candidate was successful with women in college. If he was, he hired him. As he said to me, "I know one thing for certain. If you cannot sell yourself, you sure as hell cannot sell a copier."

Xerox treated me better than any other company. Respect for people was endemic. One of my greatest honors was being invited as a special guest as one of three Whites at the annual meeting of the Bay Area Black Employees. Nearly 25 percent of the employees of Xerox at the time were Black. Diversity was not a slogan but a reality. Study after study had shown that diverse teams did much better at problem-solving. Assumptions are the source of many errors, and diverse teams challenge assumptions.

While I was treated well, I worked very hard. As part of standard management review, I was told I was going to be at corporate headquarters in Stamford for at least two more years. As a result, I sold my condominium in New York and bought a home in Norwalk, Connecticut, a few miles away from headquarters. I was glad to no longer have a long commute. Little did I realize what was going to happen.

Lyndon Hadden was the vice president of business planning for the company. Today he would be called the chief product officer, but that title did not exist then. He came to my office and asked if I would be interested in being the chief product officer for the workstation business, which would mean a move to California. I said yes but I had just moved and really did not want to move again so soon. He said OK.

I left to go talk to Roger, which brought me past the men's room. Coming out of there was the CEO who came up to me and congratulated me on my move to California, saying it was great for me and the company. I went back to Lyndon who admitted it had been discussed. Days later I was in the role.

The new CEO had replaced the general manager of the division as one of his first acts. The general manager had not endeared himself to the new CEO by attacking him a few months earlier in a review meeting (with the prior CEO) for being a corporate staffer ignorant of the real world. Those of us on the corporate staff had observed that the future CEO was suddenly riding to work every day with the incumbent CEO. We took it as a clue. We did not share it.

I was in the final business review with the general manager and the new CEO. The CEO described his response to the presentation we had just seen as "utterly dismayed." The new GM was John Shoemaker, whom I knew and liked (we are still friends), but my role was awkward. I reported to Lyndon but was a dotted line to John. Lyndon did not really recognize dots.

John was the general manager, but I controlled business and product strategy, pricing, planning, marketing, and engineering priorities and had to review all that with Lyndon. Lyndon's staff meetings were Monday on the East Coast. John's were Tuesday in the Bay Area. Frequently, I had to be back on the East Coast for Wednesday. I flew a lot via cheapest coach, stayed in cheap hotels, and used cheap rental cars. The whole point of this structure was to give Lyndon and his boss, Wayland Hicks, control over the key decisions across the company. It worked, but my position was the only one requiring this amount of travel.

Wayland was the executive who executed the turnaround with System 10. I admired him greatly. He would always see you as a direct report or one level down. To keep that promise he would schedule meetings starting at 6:30 a.m. going backwards as necessary. There were 3:30 a.m. meetings. That commitment meant everything to his people.

As great as the product was, it was obvious that the workstation business had no future. Unix workstations could already do everything they could do at a much lower price point, but the Xerox software was better. Personal computers were catching up, but it would be many years before they were equal. Microsoft Word was written by the PARC developer who wrote the Xerox word processing software, so the differences were shrinking. For many, PCs were already adequate.

The Xerox environment was brilliant but completely proprietary. There was no scale. The processor was custom to Xerox and it was dated. To get the required software performance, the operating system assumed all software could be fully trusted, which meant there could be no third-party applications. We had to shut the business down, but in a way that did not strand our customers.

Central to that was a deal to port the software to Sun workstations. This was very hard, in part because every Xerox document included machine instructions for the proprietary Xerox processor. I also did a side deal to create a single board that could fit in a PC and run the existing software, and this turned out to be quite successful. Changing hardware is a lot easier than changing software.

While this was being done, I was becoming ever more involved in corporate strategy. I was the one-eyed man in the land of the blind. I often made three cross-country trips in a week. Fuji Xerox in Japan was more dependent on the workstation business than Xerox, so I was always going there as well, plus trips to the UK. I was tired.

And underpaid. Promises to change the situation were frequent but not acted upon. I liked the company, I liked the role, and I liked the people with whom I worked. But I was exhausted. I had moved to Palo Alto, and one day in 1988 as I waited for a stoplight at Foothill Expressway, Scott McNealy pulled up alongside me. He said that Joe Graziano would be calling to hire me at Sun. In a few weeks, I had an offer which I decided to accept, for reasons both personal and professional.

I told Xerox and they made it clear they did not want me to leave. They asked me to delay a month, so I was in the awkward position of having two badges for September, though only Xerox paid me. I was negotiating a patent license from Xerox to Sun for the "snoopy buss," which made it even more awkward, since I was supposed to be representing Sun as well.

Finally, on September 30, Paul Allaire, the CEO, called me to make a counteroffer. Xerox offered me a 250 percent INCREASE in pay if I would stay. Honestly, had they made that offer earlier, I probably would have taken it, but it was just too late. The next day I started at Sun.

CHAPTER 7

SUN MICROSYSTEMS (1988–1999)

THE DAY I JOINED SUN NO ONE WAS IN THE OFFICE. Everyone was at a party to celebrate the company's reaching one billion dollars in revenue. The main joke of the event was, "What is the difference between Sun and the Boy Scouts? The Boy Scouts have adult supervision." Little did I realize the import of that joke.

SUN was an acronym for the Stanford University Network, and the founder was Andy Bechtolsheim, who created the workstation while a graduate student at Stanford. He recruited Vinod Khosla as a co-founder and CEO, who in turn recruited Scott McNealy to run operations. Shortly thereafter they recruited Bill Joy to lead software as the fourth co-founder, although he was not originally badge number 4. In Andy and Bill, Sun probably had the two brightest engineers in the world at that time.

Sun was profitable in its first quarter, an unheard-of feat, especially for a hardware startup. Although it was known as a workstation company, Sun was really a software company. Its product was its operating system, SunOS, later Solaris, although it did not seem that way in the beginning. You could not get it unless you bought Sun hardware to run it. This is the model for Apple today. As a user you only see the hardware through the operating system, so the operating system is always the product.

Sun just grew. Demand seemed insatiable. Performance improvement began to slow, and the company decided it needed to switch to its own silicon, something Apple started for similar reasons a few years ago. The details do not matter here, but Sun began to evolve from using Motorola 68000 processors to its own SPARC processors based on research from the University of California, Berkeley.

UltraSPARC II (1996)

Transitions of this sort are very tricky. When you announce a new, better product, customers are reluctant to buy more of your current product. The transition was scheduled for April 1989, which was then the start of Sun's fourth financial quarter. This type of transition gained notoriety from Osborne Computers, who went bankrupt by announcing a new product while having a large inventory of the now suddenly obsolete current product.

As a growing hardware company, Sun constantly needed cash. The CFO, Joe Graziano, decided the need was shorter-term, so he chose to raise it in debt rather than equity. He could have closed the deal but stalled because he was sure interest rates were going to fall. I was doing all the business presentations to the lenders, so I was familiar with them and the process. I was soon to learn that in reality companies do not lend money to companies. People lend money to people. People do business with people. Always.

At the same time, the company had outgrown its information systems. Sun was running on MANMAN from Ask and had just outgrown it. The vice president of information technology, Mike Graves, led a process, which selected Cullinet II as the enterprise resource planning (ERP) system. Awkwardly, it ran on an IBM-like mainframe, though Sun bought a clone. More awkwardly, Sun was the only customer for Cullinet II, so Sun had to pay for a license *and* hire the programming team.

The IT team did a great job. They tested and were ready to roll, though a bit late. Unfortunately, they overlooked one thing. ERP systems run on bills of material (BOM), a listing of the parts needed to make something. MANMAN was pretty loose on the BOMs. Errors were resolved on the factory floor. Cullinet II needed 100 percent accuracy in the BOMs to get the greater efficiency it provided.

The only path that would meet the business time requirements was to make the new SPARC products only using Cullinet II. When the orders were entered, 98 percent of them had errors due to errors in the BOMs. Cullinet II was mainframe technology based on older practices and restrictions, and it had a fixed size for the error queue. The system failed. Completely. The company went public with the statement that the technology transition had failed, which forever annoyed those involved (and still does). The point of failure was that the BOMs were wrong, but the narrative sticks to this day. While this was bad, the problem was straightforward and easily fixed. The real problem was that marketing had given manufacturing a build order that made enough product to hit the revenue target even if the customers bought only Motorola or only SPARC products, completely ignoring that cash was required to buy the parts. This was supposed to be checked by finance in manufacturing, but no one wanted to be accountable for missing the revenue target.

Joe Graziano then left without notice to return to Apple for a one-million-dollar sign-on bonus, a very large amount for the time. I had gone to lunch and was on my way back to my office. I had to walk by Scott's office to do that, and he motioned for me to come in. That is when and how I found out that I was now the acting CFO—as of that instant. I walked over to the adjacent building, which housed the finance team, and found our assistant treasurer (there was no treasurer). He had a hand-drawn chart on his desk that showed a red line crossing zero in October. My heart sinking, I asked what that October date was, and he said, "bankruptcy."

Scott was a great evangelist of the phrase, "To ask permission is to seek denial." My corporate experience to date had been at McGraw-Hill and Xerox, where such a thought was near treasonous. I was trying to adapt, but suddenly we had to impose martial law. I soon found that we had no idea what revenue had been booked until the end of the quarter. Expense controls were minimal. All that had to change.

Tony Scott, who later went on to a great career at GM, Microsoft, VMWare, and as CTO of the US government, implemented a travel tool for me in a few days to intelligently manage travel requests. The money was not really controlling, but the travel tool sent an effective message that cash mattered. Capital spending was stopped, although David Yen, who ran server engineering, came to me asking for $5 million to keep his projects going. Fortunately, I gave it to him—his work made the next decade for Sun. There are always exceptions. In a few days the IT team hacked a system that let us get a daily revenue total.

But I spent a lot of time with the banks. Eventually, the majority stood with us, and I learned once again the power of relationships. To get the funding, we needed a clean SEC form 10-K, which required our accounting firm, Ernst and Young, to issue an opinion letter without qualification that we might not be a going concern (jargon for "did we have enough cash to survive?").

Our usually very supportive EY (formerly Ernst and Young) partner said he could not do that until we got the money, which he knew we could not get until we had the letter. Literally, the company and thousands of jobs were at risk in this catch-22. Our two Goldman Sachs partners sitting in the room said they would guarantee the money. We all knew that two GS partners legally bound the firm—and with that the EY partner relented but made extensive notes saying he was holding them liable. I left to fly overnight to New York. Alone I went to Goldman Sachs to meet our attorney, who took me through signing three feet of documents. The immediate crisis was over, but all I could feel was alone.

The next two years were a whirlwind. We had a favorable deal with AT&T to put stock to them up to $25 million a quarter. All we had to do was send them a fax and they sent us $25 million for common stock priced at the closing price that day. The AT&T staff hated the deal. Joe Graziano is to be complimented for negotiating it. There was a limit, and we needed more.

Our next major crisis was strawberries. I am not making this up. To make our next financial quarter, we needed to ship product to Japan and get it out to customers. That required flying the systems to Japan. But perishable goods took precedence for air freight, and strawberries were in season. Japan eats lots of strawberries. Our products were sitting at the airport, delayed in favor of the fruit. Standing in a room and explaining this to a bunch of skeptical bankers was difficult. You could see them all thinking how they would have to repeat it to their bosses and not liking the thought. However, we made it with no time to spare, and after that there was never much doubt.

Except an earthquake. With Carol Bartz, our powerhouse sales head, and a few others, I was on tour selling a convertible bond. This is the usual financial instrument for a company in our situation, but we needed a twist. The bond has an option to convert it into equity at a fixed price. Because of the contract with AT&T, we had made a promise not to sell equity below $25 per share, which was the last price they paid. This was too high for the convertible bond market pricing, so we had to sell the bonds at a discount. This was novel at the time, but this "Sun structure" became routine.

On the road show, we were rushing to make a connection in New York for a flight to Chicago. I used the time to talk to Terry Lenaghan, our workhorse controller. During the call he said that everything was shaking, and then the call went dead. I boarded the flight with concerns. Only when we landed in Chicago were we able to learn that the factory was fine and production could resume shortly, although that Loma Prieto earthquake inflicted substantial damage on the area.

The next years were primarily about execution. Kevin Melia joined Sun from DEC to be the new CFO but agreed to spend two years running operations, which he did superbly. John Doerr, the prominent venture capitalist, was a great fan of RONABIT, the return on net assets before interests and taxes, and the compensation committee of the board, which he chaired, made that the principal metric for incentive compensation.

The company rallied around RONABIT; the competitive spirit liked winning no matter what the metric. We killed it. But in retrospect that may not have been as good as we thought. Sun shipped more than half of total revenue in the last week of each quarter and sometimes more than a quarter on the last day! This was the strategy to maximize RONABIT.

To make all this work, Kevin hired Bob Graham as his head of information technology. Officially, functional heads reported to both the functional head and the operating head, with the function having the tiebreaker. Kevin never really accepted that model, and Bob did what Kevin wanted. The short-term results were great. We largely eliminated our need for cash and reduced our total cycle time to thirty-three days with thirty-day payment terms. Technology was a substitute for cash. Later on, however, these short-term hacks greatly complicated the transition to a replacement ERP.

At Scott's initiative, we then started to focus on quality.

We met with FedEx and Motorola, then considered the leaders, as well as Xerox. As an alumnus of Xerox, I was convinced immediately. This changed the culture and contributed massively to our success in Japan. Little things matter so much. Bob Graham changed the systems to put the name and address of the customer on the product during manufacturing, and quality went up dramatically. People do business with people.

The next great step forward in the business model came from Tom Meredith, whom I had hired away from Ed Thompson, the CFO at Amdahl, as our treasurer. Tom was smart and ambitious and went on to great success at Dell. His huge contribution to Sun came in changing our model for tax. Eventually, Ed repaid the favor by suggesting Tom to Dell, which hired him away.

Crawford Beveridge was the vice president of corporate resources, which included facilities, and a huge fan of Scotland, where he later ran business development. Unsurprisingly, the Sun factory was in Linlithgow, the birthplace of Mary, Queen of Scots. It was a great facility with a great team.

In Europe, our local companies were all standalone subsidiaries, which meant they originated value on which they were taxed. They were relatively large companies for each country. There is an alternate commissionaire structure in which local companies are only undisclosed sales agents and earn only a sales commission on revenue. This legal structure effectively allows a company to locate its profits almost anywhere.

Tom went to see the tax people in the Netherlands to see if we could get any incentives for locating our distribution center there. The answer was no, because of the Treaty of Rome, which created the European Union. He thanked the people for their time and got up to leave, but the official stopped him. He said that he was also the deputy head of taxes for the Netherlands Antilles and could offer us a tax break there.

Tom pointed out that the Caribbean is not a good location for us, and the official said it was not a problem if we were a Dutch company with fiscal unity with a company in the Netherlands Antilles formed prior to the Treaty of Rome. He then handed over a list of more than 600 such companies we could buy. The Dutch obviously think ahead.

Shortly thereafter, Sun Microsystems BV existed prior to the Treaty of Rome with fiscal unity with a subsidiary in the Netherlands Antilles. We then transferred ownership of half of Sun intellectual property to that subsidiary and were allowed to depreciate it against our profits in the Netherlands. By use of the commissionaire structure, we were able to locate all profits outside the United States into the Netherlands, tax on which was then shielded by the depreciation.

The detail that allowed this was that Sun Microsystems BV had to have exactly twenty employees. At twenty, the United States considered it a factory, and so it could create value. However, Europe required twenty-one for that to be true, so to Europe it was a distribution center. This was all legal. Indeed, we were aided and abetted by government in doing it. The Netherlands gained a large distribution center with hundreds of jobs and other revenue. By the way, there was no tax shelter on Dutch profits. Later, Sun estimated this shelter was worth about $1.4 billion in cash.

Making this all happen was not easy. The country

managers suddenly saw their revenues collapse, which reduced their sense of importance. All the information technology systems had to be redone. Business process had to be totally reengineered. And hundreds of pages of contracts had to be written and executed between the various subsidiaries of the company. But $1.4 billion is $1.4 billion.

We got good at reengineering the company. Reengineering the systems for service generated large amounts of new revenue by finding unbilled services. However, when it came to the ERP systems themselves, we had much less success.

The sales force decided to start selling on the basis that we ran Sun on Sun. We did. Scott mandated that, and we had a great information technology organization, Sun Information Resources. We could recruit and retain great talent, many of whom hoped to transfer into the product or sales groups. We were cutting edge. We created the first global IP network so everyone in the company was online. The internet was not a thing yet, but we had our own.

We had one eyesore: Cullinet II running on an IBM-compatible mainframe. It really was not Cullinet II anymore, however. It had been customized extensively, but the hacks were not well documented. We really did not know how it worked. Data fields often were mislabeled.

I met the late Leon Williams in 1983, when he was CEO of Monchik-Weber, which we acquired at McGraw-Hill to be the foundation of our electronic distribution platform. Leon never went to college and was a little ashamed of that, but it did not hold him back. He had the patent on publish-and-subscribe data distribution I mentioned earlier. Using that, Monchik-Weber enabled real-time computation of stock market indices, the foundation of all modern finance. I hired him as head of information resources for SMCC, the Sun Microsystems Computer Company, and it fell to him to make the transition off the mainframe. We built the plan on publish and subscribe to lots of skepticism around what we called the Information Highway. We failed multiple times, something not actually uncommon. An ERP transition is hard.

We were moving to run on Oracle, one of our largest partners. Larry Ellison, the founder and CEO of Oracle, went to Scott to tell him to fire me because publish and subscribe was so stupid. A year later he invited me to keynote an Oracle conference on the benefits of publish and subscribe. Years after I left, Sun evaluated migrating off the Information Highway but abandoned that effort.

The technology worked fine. The problem with the effort was never technology. It was detail and people. I asked Bob Quinn, one of the best people who ever worked for me, to leave a role at service (which he had successfully reengineered) to lead the effort, Leon having left for a CTO role at Citibank. Bob made it happen, inevitably breaking some glass along the way. After I left, my successor pushed him out.

The key was taking a former controller and making her the project lead. This was as much an operations and finance project as technology, so having technology lead it was counterproductive. It took grit, determination, and intense focus on detail.

"Running Sun on Sun" proved to be a winning sales strategy, and the Sun Information Resources organization became a marketing organization. My colleagues constantly complained about the cost, but those who left invariably lamented not having what it provided. We did annual benchmarks, which showed we were comparatively very efficient, but nothing would ever satisfy them. Requirements drove the cost, not inefficiency. The sales force recognized our efforts by giving me an award at the annual sales club.

Success gave us time to reflect, and in 1992 Eric Schmidt, then the CTO of Sun, and Wayne Rosing, then head of engineering, joined me in a planning exercise. We were running on our own silicon and operating system, both of which implied a large and growing R&D expense stream. We concluded quickly that without larger volumes we would soon be unable to afford the technologies that were giving us success.

The next five or six years were consumed with trying for more volume. The first effort happened over the Christmas holidays of 1991. In a series of meetings at Scott's home, he sketched out a plan to sell our core technology to third parties and reorganize the company into five operating companies that everyone called planets: one to sell our silicon, one to sell our software, one to sell the software we built around our software, one to build and sell our computers, and one to go direct to consumers (Sun Express).

I need to digress a moment to talk about the Sun sales force. The head of sales from $100 million to $19 billion in revenue was the same person, Joe Roebuck, who has received too little recognition for his central role at the company. His contribution is of the same order as Andy Bechtolsheim or Bill Joy, but in a company that revered R&D he did not get the same reverence.

Joe was a master at recruiting, managing, and pruning a

sales force. After your initial period, if you missed your numbers for a quarter you were on probation. A second quarter and you were gone. No questions asked. No quarter given. He was careful never to build friendships with people he might have to fire. He was genius at mastering sales spiffs and the annual sales club for salespeople who met their annual goal. His other major, unheralded accomplishment, however, was resourcing. He gave every two sales reps three sales engineers; our competitors gave one. They wondered why we won.

Right after I joined, Sun held its sales conference at the Marriott in Palm Springs. Under IRS rules, a formal business purpose is required, and for that Joe hired a team-building expert. She used an animal as a foil in her presentation, and after interviewing people in the sales force, she told Joe she was going to use "junkyard dog" for that foil. Now, that was a common description of the sales force, many of whom had been at Data General Corporation prior to Sun, which had a similarly aggressive culture. Joe said absolutely not, and they "compromised" on a camel.

In the 1880s, the US Army had evaluated using camels instead of horses before rejecting the idea, but that meant camels were available in Palm Springs. One was secured and brought to the hotel for the conference.

The next morning, as Scott was rushing to catch a plane, the hotel manager was chasing him, but Scott told him to call Joe Roebuck. Thus, at 7 a.m. Joe was awakened with a query about whether he knew anything about the dead camel now floating in the hotel swimming pool. Apparently, some had taken up betting on camel racing by night, and the poor camel had fallen into the swimming pool. Camels have many strengths, but swimming is not one of them. I guess there was not a lot of water in New Mexico 40 million years ago. The hotel had to get a crane, remove the camel, then repeatedly drain, scrub, and refill the pool. Joe, of course, denied any knowledge (he always went to bed early on these nights), but Sun was banned from Marriott hotels for ten years. The story became a legend.

The sales force never accepted the concept of the planets. Their actions went beyond malicious compliance to sabotage. They were paid on commissions, and anything that lowered those by even a penny was abhorrent, regardless of the long-term consequences for the company.

Planets ended up focusing the company internally. The old Xerox joke about the man under the streetlight searching for keys he had lost across the street because the light was better applied. Transfer prices were too important. Real commerce never evolved, except with one company, Fujitsu. More on that later.

Retail was the obvious path to volume, and there was an obvious target in 1995: Apple. Under John Scully, Apple had created many differentiated versions of its core products in a hunt for more revenue. They began to sell through retail stores—the channel.

Scully was gone, and Mike Spindler was CEO. He had an impossible job. Manufacturing was out of control. Their supply chain was six months: parts had to be ordered six months before sales. Scully had left the company with fifty-three motherboards (the main part of a computer) matched by fifty-three separate versions of the operating system, then (as now again) known as MacOS. The computers used Motorola chips, which were losing to RISC. In July, Spindler had to fix the mix of products consumers would buy through the channel at Christmas among fifty-three different products. No one could do that.

A marriage with Sun had much to recommend it. Apple could use both SPARC chips and Solaris software. Apple skills on user interface and consumer packaging would be greatly helpful. Their people, the few who knew, were enthusiastic for it. The Sun people were maybe less so, but the rumors certainly got us attention.

That Christmas was due diligence for me, and it was immediately obvious that they were in trouble. Apple products sold well that Christmas, but like Sun in 1989 the mix was wrong. The channel had the right to return unsold products, and no one had a clue what that really meant.

We had our joint meeting at Wilson Sonsini, our law firm, and Scott asked Eff Martin, our Goldman Sachs banker, to present our bid. He did so most reluctantly, but we were the customer. At that time, Apple was trading around $28 per share, and normal expectations for a takeover would be a premium of 30 percent or so. This meant Apple was expecting a price of $35 or so. We offered half that: $18. At that point, Frank Quattrone, their banker, who had the reputation as the best banker in the business, threw his yellow legal pad into the air.

Nevertheless, they took it. Apple later traded down much lower, and their survivability was in doubt. I got the signed contract from Mike Markula, the chairman of the board, a little after 1 a.m., and went back to meet Scott, Larry Sonsini, John Doerr, and the Wilson Sonsini litigator, who was brought into the conversation for the first time. The Sun board had approved, so Scott had the authority to sign.

The litigator went ballistic. The idea of buying a major public company below market was, he thought, just insane. Lawsuits would be filed immediately, and because of the way the law works, Sun would own those lawsuits. He did not believe any judge would let us invoke the *force majeure* clause (which lets you exit an agreement if something unexpected occurs) even if it was justified. I returned the contract, and we all went home.

The Apple board then made Gil Amelio the CEO. Gil did a lesser version of this deal eventually by buying NeXT from Steve Jobs for $400 million (more on that later). That of course brought Steve back into Apple, and the rest is history.

What would we have done? I don't know. Scott had picked Ed Zander, who ran software at Sun, to be the CEO of Apple if we bought them. He is a good friend, a good executive, and a great marketer. But retail would have been all new, and he struggled with that later when he was CEO at Motorola, because it was a new business. The synergies were enormous, and without consumer volumes, Sun had problems reaching sustainability.

A year later we made a less intensive run at buying Packard Bell, then a booming PC maker. The fit was much less attractive, but the price was also much lower. As part of that effort, I went to Sacramento to inspect their new factory there. It looked clean, which it was, because that factory was only operating for the one hour I was there visiting, though it was used more later. This is a deal I am happy we did not do.

We put a lot of effort into running Solaris on Intel. Fearing that the normal antibodies would kill the effort, we located the Intel effort near Boston and set out to build an Intel workstation running Solaris. We built a good product, but it never got volume. It was an orphan in our product line, and people were buying Solaris, not SPARC or Intel.

I did spend one Christmas Eve in my home study with John Miner, then an executive vice president of Intel. We had exchanged drafts of a patent cross-license, essential for us to launch the Intel product, but there were many issues left. Without lawyers, we resolved them all in a few hours, printed the contract, and signed it. A patent cross-license without any cash payments. Again—the power of relationships.

Our one success in gaining volume was Fujitsu, the largest Japanese computer company. They bought our planet story completely and also bought eventually up to a billion dollars of product annually, which they sold under their name. This was an incredibly profitable business, and without it the history of Sun would have been very different.

Seeing how important and yet how different the Japanese companies were, Scott gave me a collateral duty of executive contact for Fujitsu, Toshiba, and C. Itoh, companies that in total were over 20 percent of our revenue and a much larger percentage of our profit. To help me, I hired Kei Honda as the chairman of Sun Japan.

Kei had no management responsibility. There was a vice president for Japan who managed the day-to-day business. Kei had one job: make sure we did business with them the way they wanted. Relationships.

Fujitsu took most of our time. With all three companies I applied the rule book I had learned at Xerox. We had an annual summit, quarterly steering committee meetings, and monthly status checks. We alternated venues. Sun people were generally reluctantly supportive, because they knew the business importance, but this was not a way of making friends inside the company.

Sekizawa-san was the *Sacho* of Fujitsu. We translate this as CEO, but it is really *leader*, and he shares power with five deputy leaders (*Fucho Sacho*) who report to him sort of, as they are directly elected by the shareholders. He was very smart and understood the strengths and weaknesses of Fujitsu.

At one meeting I had talked about kernel-capable software engineers, engineers good enough that they could work on the UNIX kernel, the hardest part of the operating system. We had a study done that estimated there were fewer than 800 such engineers in the world. We employed roughly 550 of them. Sekizawa made Fujitsu count: they had 3.

My counterpart at Fujitsu was Ohtsuki-san, one of the finest men I met in my career, and a Fucho Sacho at Fujitsu. On a tourist visit to Japan in 2019 to show the country to my grandnephew, I was delighted that Ohtsuki joined us for dinner. At one point we were incredibly dependent on the supply of a particular microprocessor from Fujitsu. We were going to miss our quarter badly if they did not deliver.

Ohtsuki took a day from his schedule and drove to the plant. He told the plant manager he had given his word they would deliver. Then left. That was all he had to do. I later learned that they set up a regular convoy to test the chips in another location to meet our deadline. Relationships. For that favor I took him to his favorite restaurant. Dinner for four was $6,000 (over twenty years ago), but that was cheap.

Toshiba was an easier partner than Fujitsu because they did not consider themselves a leader in R&D. Relationships were critical, however, so one day I flew to Japan from California, landed at 3:30 p.m., reached the Four Seasons hotel at 6:55, said "Kompai!" (Cheers!) at 7:01, and was headed back to the airport by 7:05 for the 10 p.m. flight home. We were celebrating ten years of partnership, and someone of equal rank had to be there from Sun. As the party was all in Japanese, my leaving was not important. My momentary presence was.

In my time, we had two other relationship challenges with Toshiba. Once, after our meeting ended, the CEO unusually walked toward the elevator with Scott. Since this was behind me, I did not notice it, and when I got to the elevator, I pushed the button. This required me to write a long and sincere letter of apology to the CEO, as in his presence only he can push the elevator button.

I was told that in Japan business cards are graded 0-63 based on size, card stock, embossing, rounded or square corners, and other physical attributes. This allows someone to quickly compute his or her standing versus another without looking at the card and then to bow appropriately based upon the difference in grade. The CEO of Toshiba is a 63.

The other challenge came later when a successor CEO, Saito, who had been very helpful to us on quality, announced that he wanted to visit our plant in Scotland. I received a side message that he was looking forward to playing golf at St. Andrews, which is nearby.

St. Andrews was claimed by the state hundreds of years ago, and access is controlled nominally by lottery. However, whoever ran that lottery knew we were the largest employer in the county, so that was not an obstacle. But that was irrelevant. The Saturday that he wanted to play happened to be the day of the annual tournament of the Royal and Ancient, the founding golf club of golf, whose home course is St. Andrews.

I talked to my contact at Toshiba, who politely told me he was sorry I had such a big problem, but that if we could not find a way for him to play there on that day, our relationship would be damaged forever. Crawford Beveridge came to the rescue. He discovered that there were two tee times not taken by the tournament, which went to members based on seniority. The payment of a gratuity to an eighty-three-year-old member secured the second of those tee times, so we were set. I happily called back my contact, who thanked me and then said Saito would play with his colleagues at Gleneagles. Relationships.

We looked at buying other revenue streams as local national computer companies struggled: ICL in the UK and Bull in France. There was really no fit with either, but we spent time on them. There was one struggling company that looked potentially attractive: NeXT, founded by Steve Jobs. We evaluated the company in depth.

NeXT made a great product, but it had limited market acceptance. Their largest source of revenue was Credit Suisse, and I met the person there writing the checks. He told me that they made over $450 million a year in trading profits because his team could write software faster using NeXT than his competitors using something else. So he kept NeXT alive.

What NeXT had was great software built around a great language based on what was known as the Mach kernel. That kernel was written by Avie Tevanian as a graduate student at Carnegie Mellon, and it was fantastic. Avie was the head of software at NeXT, followed Steve to Apple to run software there, and created OS/X, the foundation of all Apple software today.

Smartphones existed before the iPhone, but writing applications for them was difficult. Applications had to be phone-call aware, as they could be interrupted at any point. The Nokia 95 was a wonderful device. The software was very weak. What Avie recognized was that once the microprocessor speed reached 700 MHz, you could use a computer operating system with voice just as an application. That is the key insight of the iPhone. That is the insight Eric Schmidt took from Apple to buy Android at Google.

Steve wanted $400 million for NeXT. He knew it was high and knew we were most unlikely to pay it. However, he had taken an investment from Canon at $400 million and promised them they would not lose money. We took a trip to Japan to see Canon, but while the trip gave us some memories, they were not selling for less.

I went to see Steve to give him our offer. The receptionist told me he was waiting for me in the boardroom. Although NeXT was a startup, the board room was solid mahogany and imposing. Steve was at the end of the table under a spotlight. The rest of the room was dark. Sitting in the dark, I complimented him on the latest Pixar movie, but he cut me off.

What is the number, he said. I answered $283 million. He said, "Congratulations. That is the right number. If I were Sun, that is what I would offer. I want $400." Then he walked out. So that deal did not happen either. The preceding Sunday, Steve had invited me to his house to have breakfast with his family while we discussed terms. Focus.

Volume actually came from a nonsensical sentence. We had paid a marketing consultant to help improve our messaging, and they came up with Network the Dog. We implemented it, but it was never going to change our path. We gave the dog away. Ed Zander came into our management meeting one morning and said, "I've got it." Ed's idea was, "We put the dot in dot com." Everyone understood what it meant. We connected you to the internet. Over twenty-five *Fortune* 50 CEOs called Scott's office the day the ad ran for the first time in the *Wall Street Journal*. That phrase more than doubled Sun revenues.

By then Sun was a server company supporting web services and databases. The government was a huge customer, as was the adult entertainment industry. If you wanted to build a web startup, you needed Sun. I was never so popular, as people constantly pestered me for discounts.

We had the best platform, but we lacked a lot of the tools needed to set up a web business. Then Miles Gilburne called. Miles was the senior vice president of corporate development for AOL and did their many acquisitions. A key to their success was an accounting technique called pooling of interest.

If two companies merged using all stock and followed a set of complex rules, the accounting was done as if the companies had been merged from day one. Cisco also employed this. Mergers just disappeared except for some additional shares. This helped make the financial statements very attractive. Presumably, this is why this technique is no longer allowed.

AOL wanted to buy Netscape, but did not want its enterprise business. However, to do this and keep pooling of interest was very complicated. Miles and I spent weeks working out the structure, which ended up being a joint venture that eventually defaulted to Sun. Technically, AOL always had a tie vote, but they had to pay Sun $5 million each time they used it.

David Colburn, the AOL head of business development, and I negotiated the deal over a hectic week and weekend. We got it done or almost done. He left before we were finished because of a prior commitment, but he left me the signature pages. His attorney was furious, but David thought I knew the deal better and would protect him more. There were really only details to sort, and their attorney, Gio Hunt, was more than capable. However, I appreciated the gesture.

That let me get to know AOL, and they got to know me. Scott decided to turn over more control of Sun to Ed Zander, which left me in an awkward place, so when Miles called me, I took the call.

As I look back at my time at Sun, what I remember most, as do most alumni, is the people. The talent at Sun was simply incredible. Bill Joy's law (the number of really bright people at a company is proportional to the log of the number of employees, so the percentage of really bright people declines rapidly with size) was broken at Sun for a long time. Growth enabled that, but so did the management philosophy.

Scott has never gotten credit for the management practices at Sun, which Eric Schmidt later took to Google. Central to everything was a doctrine of Architect and Distribute, which is reproduced in full in Appendix 2 at the end of this book. The idea was to push decision-making out as far as possible. Loosely coupled but highly aligned was the goal.

To do that you needed rules, and architects set those rules. Scott lived by defining his role as deciding who decides. We minimized the number of rules. If we were not going to fire someone for breaking a rule, we did not have it.

Alignment was an overriding goal. Instant email everywhere in the world was part of it (and unique at the beginning). Emails elsewhere could and sometimes did take days back then. Frequent in-person meetings so employees could see and interact with their leadership were required. Scott believed fervently in the concept "all the wood be behind one arrowhead," so annually he would set a target all could understand.

Another powerful tool was so simple: the corporate calendar. We set it out a year in advance. Every month included a travel week when no corporate meetings were allowed, so people could plan international travel (and vacations). We had a corporate week when corporate meetings could be held and you were supposed to be around. Management meetings were set. We changed it as rarely as we could once published.

We had a planning process that I largely copied from Xerox. We started the first days after Christmas break with a meeting to decide on the earnings-per-share target for the next year. These were sometimes contentious, but they put a marker in the sand. We then ran a series of other meetings to convert this into a detailed plan. The work this required was not popular, so we assigned it to a team of vice presidents. This taught them the necessity of the effort, and they became supportive.

We also had a set of ten corporate goals to which management compensation was tied. Scott had a rule that for every goal there had to be a clear-cut way to determine whether it was met, and the attainment was audited by the audit committee of the board. All executives working for Scott were on the same goals, a source of constant annoyance but effective.

The rubric I sold was that a company was nothing but a cascade of bargains, and business success and employee satisfaction both required that those bargains be kept. That took planning. This complemented our overall focus on quality.

The result of this management process was a highly talented, highly dedicated, and hugely supportive workforce. The year I was acting head of people I did the math and decided to close the company for most employees from Christmas through New Year's. The impact on lives was stunning. This Christmas break was cited again and again as the number one reason for staying at Sun, because in the always-on culture of Silicon Valley, it was really a break. Other companies followed suit.

Wayne Rosing is probably best known as the first vice president of engineering at Google, but he brought enormous value to Sun by showing us how to best manage talent. He launched Sun Labs as a magnet to attract great talent that did not want to deal with the business aspects of technology. We limited it to 100 people and required that if they wanted to stay with their idea, they had to leave the Labs and join the product group bringing it to market.

More importantly, Wayne brought us the concept of Distinguished Engineer. These were the slightly more than 100 top engineers at Sun. They were paid and had the same status as a director-level executive, a job that paid $300 to $500 thousand a year at that time, with eligibility for bonuses that could bring in a few million dollars. A DE could not be assigned to work on anything, but they had to be working full-time on projects of their choice. Thus, management could quickly judge the quality of an effort by how many DEs were working on it. Most importantly, only the DEs by vote could make someone a DE. Management had no say in the process.

We all understood that our success rested on the talents of a very small number of engineers, and we did everything we could to beat Bill Joy's law. Rapid growth made that easy for a while, but Wayne's contributions were key. Top management spent a lot of time recruiting and retaining talent. When James Gosling threatened to quit over a strategy disagreement, Scott offered to let him stay to work on whatever he wanted. As CFO, I signed a lease for a building I knew nothing about, including its address. Out of that effort came Java, which propelled Sun for years.

My biggest frustration was personal productivity tools. The ones we had were just not that good. The standard was Microsoft Office and displacing it was impossible. When I joined, Sun had a team writing its own suite, but we decided to kill it because application developers saw it as a sign we might compete with them, so it was hurting our overall evangelism effort.

We did buy three companies along the way that brought us office suites, but none achieved real traction. The last one, Star Office, still lives on as LibreOffice. It never achieved the goals we had for it, but the day we bought it the market value of Sun went up over a billion dollars for a $57 million acquisition. It certainly helped shareholder value. The CEO of the first company we bought was Jonathan Schwartz, who later became the CEO of Sun. While these tools mattered to Scott and to me, the reality was the executives running them did not prioritize them.

We spent a lot of money and effort on something we called WABI, the Windows Application Binary Interface, intended to allow Windows software to run on Solaris on Intel. Without cooperation from Microsoft, we knew this was going to be very hard. It turned out to be impossible. We got very close, but it could never be enough. Microsoft documentation was all stored in a proprietary application we could not support, and without documentation the effort was doomed. We tried to do a deal with IBM (who wanted WABI maybe more than we did), but we could not find terms.

In the open-source world of today, it would have been easy, but not then.

Lots of lessons. We were ahead of our time in management philosophy. Included at the end of this book as Appendix 3 is a 1993 discussion of how we managed change, which I HIGHLY suggest you read. It is still state of the art.

While I really enjoyed my roles and had my frustrations in all of them, the role that changed me most was my year as acting head of human resources. No one wanted me in that job. Certainly not my colleagues. Even more so the HR staff. In the end, however, we all got along. Years later I was told the HR staff voted me the best head of HR in their tenure, but this may have been a deliberate knock on my successor.

My primary assignment was finding and hiring my successor, but we had our share of HR issues. HR included facilities, and one day the vice president in charge asked me to accompany him to a lunch with the mayor of a city where we were trying to build a new facility. For some reason, we were having trouble getting permits. The mayor turned out to be a friend of mine from high school, so the permits arrived that afternoon. I had no idea he was the mayor, but my vice president was annoyed I had not told him earlier.

We had multiple campuses around the world, and (much as at Data Resources) even though they shared common management and policies, productivity and culture varied widely among them. Some never clicked and never shipped product. None were as good as the core engineering campus. We tried to figure it out, but I could never find a simple answer. Maybe it was just that the campus strongly affected who applied to work there.

Some campus differences were obvious. All-employee meetings on the West Coast looked like a meeting of the United Nations. Not so on the East Coast. Overall, we had three persistent diversity issues: (1) women in senior management, (2) women in engineering, and (3) Black people overall. My time at Harvard and Xerox made me a firm believer in diversity, and I spent a lot of time and effort on the subject.

The women of Sun were and are an unrecognized source of strength. They made Sun as much as any group. At the last reunion, Carol Bartz led a well-deserved shoutout. About half of our director roles in the mid-1990s were filled by women. This was pretty unusual. These were jobs with total compensation up to $500,000 per year, and we had very few vice presidents for a company of our size. However, women were underrepresented in those ranks. Many of our women directors told us they did not want the tradeoffs required. While vice presidents did make more, they worked and traveled a lot more.

Our top engineers were overwhelmingly male. The demographic data suggested there were very few women in the labor pool, and Sun engineering was incredibly merit-based. You did not perform, and you were gone. Remember, Distinguished Engineers elected new ones. Poll after poll found that we were not prejudiced against women. However, the polls suggested we were prejudiced against femininity. We probably were.

Black employees were definitely underrepresented. This was totally different than at Xerox. I hired multiple consultants to help us identify any root cause, but we continued to struggle. I thought we made extra effort, but maybe we were different.

We did lead in one area: transgender. During my tenure, three employees transitioned from one gender to another, and I don't remember that it was really a big deal. At that time, you needed certification from a psychiatrist, and the process took at least a year. Transitions were very expensive, and while we did not cover them up front, once you had the certification, you could gain coverage on appeal. In general we were way ahead on so many issues. Our policies would still be current today, maybe even liberal.

The reason human resources was so fascinating to me is that it was clear attracting and retaining talent was the key strategic challenge, and in that competition every little detail matters. I learned that again in many one-on-one recruiting efforts. Bad hires hurt everyone—especially the employee.

However, for me in 1999, I had learned about all that I

was going to learn at Sun. It was time to let a new team take over my roles. I had nowhere else to go there, so it was time to move on to a new company.

CHAPTER 8

POTS AND THE INTERNET

T'S PROBABLY BEST IF I PROVIDE A LITTLE BACKGROUND ON WHAT THE INTERNET LOOKED LIKE IN 1999. Led by AT&T and Bell Laboratories, the world telephone industry did a remarkable thing for its time: created a telephone network that spanned the globe and delivered amazing reliability. Calls worked 99.999 percent of the time or more. You could hear the party on the other end. Phones worked even if the power failed. We call this network, unfairly, POTS, for Plain Old Telephone Service.

As I was leaving Harvard, a friend set me up for an interview at Bell Laboratories. The trick interview question was, "What is 10 cents?" The answer was $100 million. The math was that 10 cents a month on handset rentals was $100 million a year to AT&T. That was the business model.

The phone in your home or on your desk was connected to a copper wire, and that wire went all the way back to a central office where it was connected to a big switch, which was really a computer with lots of ports. By the 1990s, these switches were 5ESSs (fifth-generation electronic switching systems). Central offices were large, secure, windowless computer rooms. Each wire carried electric power as well to power the phone (which limited the number of phones one line could support).

Your phone number was really a short program. Dialing "1" switched you to a different computer; the next three digits said what remote switch you went to (area code); that switch determined which switch processed the rest of the number by the next three digits; and that switch then handled the last four. This is the North American Numbering Plan. Other areas had similar plans. This all worked long before we had the hardware and software we take for granted today. Numbers were locked to physical hardware and were assigned that way.

When the government mandated that phone numbers be portable across carriers, Neustar was born, founded by the staffers who wrote the regulations. Thereafter, calls to ported numbers went to Neustar to see who now owned the number and route it accordingly, making Neustar a very profitable company.

Timesharing was the way computers were first accessed remotely starting in the mid-1970s. Computers were still mainframes, huge boxes in big computer rooms, but they could be shared. My first remote connection was a teletype on wheels with an acoustic coupler into which you stuck a telephone handset. Modems converted electrical signals into tones, which went over the telephone line to another modem that converted them back. It was magic. Initial speeds were slow and eventually maxed out at 56 kilobits per second.

For this to work, you needed inbound modems, so to

offer the service a company had to lease telephone lines across the country wherever it wanted to offer service. At the time, long-distance calls, especially what were called local long-distance, were very expensive, so you had to be local. However, in North America outbound calls were in general unlimited for a monthly fee. I learned all this at Data Resources years before the internet. This was the state of online connectivity until the arrival of broadband.

Telephone companies were regulated, and their largest asset was the wired plant—the wires that ran to the central offices from homes and buildings. At AT&T, this asset was managed by the corporate treasury department and was depreciated over forty years. Sadly, when AT&T was broken up, this department was abolished as it had no owner, so the local telephone companies literally had no idea what wires went where. Modifications were made daily, so the original maps became obsolete.

The telephone industry attempted to innovate. In 1988, they launched ISDN, Integrated Services Digital Network. Work had started all the way back in 1980, and by the time it was launched it was too late. It never got traction. A startup, Jetstream, introduced a consumer product that fully exploited the features. I owned one and loved it, but I was the exception. The maximum data speed was either 128 or 112 kbps, depending on the local implementation, which was obsolete almost from the beginning.

The other huge, wired network was cable television. This was organized much the same way, as required by the laws of physics. Central offices were called *headends*, and served the same purpose as in telephony. TV was a broadcast medium, and the copper wiring created a private radio network over which to broadcast. There needed to be repeaters along the way.

Things got more complicated as the commercial offerings got more complicated. HBO introduced the idea of pay television, and the ability to watch had to be limited to those who subscribed. This introduced encrypted content, which meant it had to be decrypted. This brought about set-top boxes, which were computers sitting at the end of the copper cable. By 2000, set-top boxes were among the most complicated, if not the most complicated, consumer electronics devices in the market.

Vint Cerf and Bob Kahn are credited with developing the set of protocols known as TCP/IP, Transmission Control Protocol and Internet Protocol, which today define communications on the internet. They are among the most brilliant inventions of our time, and they have scaled from thousands of users to billions remarkably well. They have little in common with telephony or cable television.

"The internet" is a common phrase today, but virtually no one understands what that means. If you are interested, read the report of the Committee on Internet Navigation and Domain Name Services of the National Academy of Sciences (I was a member of that committee).

There is a group of major telecommunications companies who have agreed to share traffic among themselves (tier 1 providers) and to operate their networks using TCP/IP. These players agree to settlement-free peering, meaning that they do not charge each other for traffic. They do charge other players who connect to them. To avoid collisions, these players each have an allocation of IP addresses they got from a non-profit corporation, the American Registry of Internet Numbers (or a similar organization in other areas).

Originally, the ultimate authority was the US Department of Commerce, which transferred that to a California not-for-profit corporation, the Internet Corporation for Assigned Names and Numbers (ICANN). ICANN runs the naming and numbering system for the internet, and the tier 1 providers agree to use that. That's it. That's the internet.

The beauty of this design is that people do not need to deal with the numbers. Instead, there is another complex network called the Domain Name System, which functions to convert alphanumeric addresses into the numbers. Central to this system are thirteen root servers. Your computer, phone, or other device has software called a DNS resolver, and you need to give it the numeric address of a DNS server. The resolver takes the alphanumeric address and passes it to the DNS server, which returns a numeric address. To do that, it first goes to a root server, which has a fixed numeric address.

The root server looks at the last part of the address and passes back the numeric address of the domain server, which handles those addresses. The server then goes to that address to get the final numeric address and passes that back to the resolver. The most common domain is .com, which has over a million addresses in it and is managed by Network Solutions, which was the initial company to set up the internet.

Fragile as it may seem, this scheme has scaled to an internet of billions of devices. Today, a lot of the intermediate players cache the addressing information to improve efficiency. This is all IP version 4. Much like ISDN, a new version

(6) has been around for a decade, but it is IPv4 that still runs the world.

Both television companies and cable TV companies raced to offer high-speed or broadband access to the internet. They owned the only usable wires to homes, though there were a few attempts to offer internet over power lines. The first cable offering (which later became known as Roadrunner) was in 1995. The science was pretty simple. The private radio space was divided into six-megahertz chunks. Chunk zero sent data out, and a home was assigned a channel to receive data. In addition to the set-top box, you now needed a cable modem, which talked to a CMTS (Cable Modem Termination System).

The telephone system did the same thing over its wires, calling it DSL, Digital Subscriber Line. Those lines connected to a DSL access multiplexor, which did the same thing as a CMTS. Unfortunately for the telephone companies, the cable companies had a thicker wire with which to work, so they had more bandwidth. It was not a battle the telephone companies could win except where they had wires and cable did not.

Companies tried to compete with wireless and satellite, and while both still survive in niches, the real battle now is in running fiber optic cables to the home. SpaceX is starting to offer a much better satellite service with Starlink, and wireless companies can be competitive as well with 5G.

However, in 1999 cable was looking more and more like an entrenched monopoly. And that brings us to AOL.

CHAPTER 9

AOL/AOL TIME WARNER (1999–2004)

A S I MENTIONED IN THE PREFACE, AOL BASICALLY WAS THE CONSUMER INTERNET IN THE 1990S.

In large part this was due to Steve Case, its chairman and CEO. Steve is a very approachable, friendly man with a relaxed manner. You liked him when you met him. He was inclusive before it was cool. He is called a founder, but legally he was hired years after the company started operation. There is no question he is the founder of what the business became, however.

What Steve possessed and still possesses is an uncanny instinct for the consumer. He knew what would work and what would not. His persistence on simplicity kept the company out of so many sand traps.

Really, for a world based on POTS communication AOL was remarkable. Step one was to get a copy of the CD with the application. Jan Brandt, the senior vice president of marketing, invented a simple strategy: carpet bombing. AOL CDs were simply everywhere. Everywhere. People joked that they were the American coaster for beverages.

AOL CDs (mid-1990s)

Once installed on your computer, you went to step two. Step two, you connected a phone line to your computer. There were thousands of possible configurations of personal computers and modems. AOL had a team of hundreds testing them and finding the incredibly arcane settings needed to dial into AOL. Almost always, the user had to do nothing more than connect the line, because the necessary settings were provided automatically.

Step three, you picked a screen name, which was freeform. Prodigy gave you a computer-generated name. CompuServe a number. At AOL you could be *bunnyrabbit3*. And that mattered. I was told that when a customer called to cancel, once they were told that someone else could get their screen name, much of the time they stopped and kept the account. People chose names that mattered to them, and they were uncomfortable with the idea of someone else having it.

Step 4 was to input your phone number. At this point, the software would dial a toll-free number to get local phone numbers and you were done except for providing a credit card. Accounts renewed automatically until canceled. This was key to the business success.

You were then at the home screen. This was always a mess to designers, but there was a method to the madness. Nearly every user could find something on which to click on the page. No searching needed. Immediate gratification. The competing Microsoft page looked beautiful, but the typical consumer faced multiple clicks to get to what they wanted. Clicks mattered.

AOL optimized itself to the dial-up internet and was rewarded accordingly. However, it may have proved to be its downfall. DNA, company DNA, is difficult to change. You have to remember that AOL was there long before there was even an internet, let alone broadband.

In 1995, Microsoft introduced Windows 95, their first graphical user interface for personal computers. That technology was decades old, having been invented at Xerox Palo Alto Research Center years earlier. However, only in 1995 did personal computers begin to have the necessary power to run such an interface effectively.

When Steve saw it, he knew it was going to be a huge hit with consumers and told Matt Korn and Gerry MacDonald, who ran operations and the network, to buy up all the inbound modem lines in the United States that they could. They told him there was no need, they had a plan to grow as needed. Steve said to just buy.

He was right. That Christmas millions of Americans got

personal computers with modems, and AOL had paid Microsoft to be installed on the home screen. AOL was just a few clicks away. Competitors rushed to add capacity, but there were no available modem lines for some time. AOL became a colossus.

Miles Gilburne opened the conversation with me to join AOL as his replacement as the head of corporate development, a role I had at Sun. It was a fascinating role. AOL had grown by acquisition, buying new capabilities and making its founders very wealthy. Miles wanted to retire, he said, and I was a candidate to replace him.

As you may expect, there were lots of interviews, and in general they were very friendly and supportive. But there was one thing I sensed immediately: the real product of AOL was its stock, and everything was run around maintaining its growth in price. As this fueled its ability to acquire at low cost, it was a viable strategy.

There was one thing I did not recognize until later. AOL was managed by two teams that co-existed, generally friendly but not always. The chief operating officer was Bob Pittman, and he ran operations. He had his own deal guy in David Colburn, and deals were a large part of making their numbers. The technology operation reported to Bob, and his team was very loyal. They all knew Steve was CEO and they respected that—but they worked for Bob.

At the time of these conversations, the CTO of AOL was Marc Andreessen, who got the job as part of the merger of Netscape into AOL. Miles, Marc, Mike Kelly (the CFO), George Vradenburg (public policy), and Ken Novack (vice chair, though not a director) reported to Steve along with

Bob. Marc was leaving, and AOL was worried about how that would be perceived by investors. Steve also had a long history with Miles and trusted him completely. He did not want him to leave.

Suddenly, there was a switch. There was no longer a vacancy in Miles's role, but AOL needed to replace Marc as CTO for image reasons. I was offered the role of chief technology officer instead. It was a very attractive offer. I was to develop AOL's broadband strategy. Spend up to two years learning the business, then return to California and build it with a new team headquartered at the Netscape campus. The pay package Steve valued at $100 million.

None of that came true. I actually lost $8 million on the stock awards that made up the vast majority of that package (for tax reasons).

But in the moment it was big news. The story made the *New York Times* and *Wall Street Journal*. I was excited to be doing something new. I found a home in Virginia, which I expected to be temporary (twenty-two years later I am still there) and started at AOL. Steve was a very hands-off boss, so I was pretty much on my own.

My first staff meeting was two weeks after I joined, and there I learned that Steve had had a change of heart. Instead of going the broadband route, at least immediately, he had decided to pursue a merger with Time Warner. I had been the corporate sponsor for them at Sun, and I found the place to be toxic. I warned Steve, but the eternal optimist that he is, he brushed away my concerns. He saw the merger as a brief delay to get a much stronger base. He told me to hang on and believe. I did. At the same time, Sun made a furtive effort to get me to return, but although Scott wanted it, the lieutenants he sent were half-hearted. I stayed.

I really did not have a job at AOL. I was well paid and well titled, but technology worked for Bob Pittman. If you did not work for him, you did not exist unless he needed you. He was not the first person like that I met in my career. My access to Steve, however, gave me the power to warn, advise, and counsel, and allowed me to be aware to inform. I also got involved on most deals. Finally, I had a small staff of smart people who could help. No one really argued that I had the assignment to develop a plan for AOL 2.0. No one else was doing it. I developed good relationships with nearly all the senior technology executives over time as well as with David Colburn and his team for deals.

AOL had a broadband access problem. The cable companies had the power position and the best broadband. The laws of physics meant that cable could offer better broadband than the telephone companies. They were always going to win. But the cable companies would not cooperate with AOL. They had no interest in sharing their customers. However, they never succeeded in developing a great product, despite countless attempts, especially by Time Warner Cable, which invented broadband over cable.

AOL did what it could and struck deals with the telephone companies for DSL access. It never really worked. A large percentage of the orders were never installed. The underlying DSL connections were not great. The telephone companies were telephone companies and inherently not great partners. With them as their sole allies, AOL was certain to lose.

George Vradenburg was very successful in spearheading an open access initiative. The goal was simple. Just as telephone companies were required to share their last-mile lines, so should cable companies. He might have succeeded had he been allowed to continue, but the merger was an alternate strategy to buy the largest cable provider of broadband. Allegro Networks even created the necessary hardware to enable easy sharing of those last-mile links. The world might be very different had open access come to fruition.

The Time Warner merger was uncertain and was going to take time, so AOL kept looking at alternatives. At the time, eBay was struggling. They had technology issues that looked really bad in the press, and Meg Whitman, the CEO, was looking for lifelines. She hired Maynard Webb to fix the problem, and he in turn hired a new team, one of whom, Bob Quinn, had worked for me at Sun.

Miles and I flew to California and met with Maynard, and it was clear immediately to us that none of these problems were insurmountable. The team in place would fix them in due course. So we started to negotiate a merger with them. Although one eBay director strongly resisted, at the time of the eventual merger with Time Warner, AOL could have chosen to merge with eBay. Given how things turned out, that would have been a much different merger. You can only speculate as to how it would have played out.

Bob Pittman had a strong desire to offer AOL radio as part of every session. It was just too expensive to do that. Every person who listened required a separate process run to generate the audio stream, even though we only offered a small number of streams.

One day, Gil Weigand and I visited Extreme Networks. Gil is a brilliant computer scientist and dedicated public servant and one of the very best employees I ever had. Wire speed is the concept that traffic can only move so fast on a network, and as computers became faster there was now an opportunity to do some processing within a network switch without slowing down the traffic. We were talking to Extreme Networks about this, when I thought that we could just use the switch to be like a copier. So was born Ultravox. Gil and a team of engineers made it reality, and the day it went live, AOL was able to replace hundreds of servers with one 8.5" x 11" card in an Extreme Networks switch.

Unfortunately, because it was so efficient the market was small, or the card was underpriced. The patents were not, however, and Time Warner eventually sold them as part of a more than one-billion-dollar transaction to Microsoft, who in turn sold them to Facebook, which continued to extend the patents for years. Had AOL been willing to exploit it, Ultravox would have enabled an incredibly strong position in streaming. An opportunity lost.

Broadband remained the conundrum. The AOL experience was optimized for dial-up. Graphics and video did not really fit that technology, but they were the consumer preference once broadband was available. The cable companies refused to partner, and the telephone companies lacked the physics to succeed. You did not have to be very smart to forecast the future.

We conceived a way around this: the ABC box (AOL Broadband Connector). The most highly rated DSL service was the one offered by DirecTV. The reason was that they installed a management layer in their software so that their customer support people could help consumers manage their broadband experience. We built on this. The idea was simple: create a device for the home connected to broadband that AOL could help you manage. It would have storage, so it could securely hold music and videos, and provide WiFi.

The hidden strength of AOL was its customer support. It was really good. All senior officers were expected to spend time each week listening in on support calls, so we understood the reality of our market. Employees were all US-based and went the extra mile. Legendary stories helped drive that culture, whether they were true or not.

The one I remember most is of the customer who called to complain that AOL had spilled her coffee. The customer support person was very patient, and she eventually learned that the customer liked her coffee-cup holder on her personal computer. Most people called it a CD-ROM drive, but it actually functioned well as a coffee-cup holder. Unfortunately, when your computer restarted, it withdrew back into the PC. AOL updated and required a restart, hence spilling the coffee. Life.

THE INTERREGNUM

Following that fateful January 2000 press conference that I described in the Preface, we went into a strange period I called the Interregnum. Everything was supposed to stay the same, but you knew everything was about to change ... maybe. Steve and Miles led the negotiations, but the final negotiations were between Steve and Jerry Levin, the CEO of Time Warner. There were no intracompany meetings, and no real due diligence, though both were public companies with full disclosure. There was no effort to build a common vision. In retrospect, the hubris on both sides was mountainous. Both Steve and Jerry had a vision for the future. In Steve's case, his team shared it. That was not true with Jerry, who had been frustrated with getting his team on board. He saw the merger with AOL as his means of making it happen. Thus, when Steve offered to have Jerry as the CEO, he grabbed it.

Although the Time Warner people always framed it as Time Warner buying AOL, AOL bought Time Warner. It was a merger of equals but with AOL shareholders getting 55 percent of the equity. The board was evenly split. Steve was chairman with some specific responsibilities, including technology. AOL executives held the CFO role, general counsel role, and public policy at corporate, and Bob Pittman and Dick Parsons were co–chief operating officers.

We learned quickly that Time Warner operated totally differently. They never held staff meetings. There was a simple legal reason for this. The heads of the divisions were not section 16(b) officers, so there was no obligation to disclose their compensation. If they met as a staff, some of them at least would arguably be 16(b). And they made a lot of money. Tens of millions of dollars per year.

The corporate staff compensation had to be disclosed. As best I could tell, they solved their compensation challenge very cleverly. They set the annual budget targets based off the first round of budget submissions from the divisions, and then provided accelerators for overachievement at the corporate level. As soon as they were set, the center constantly beat up on the divisions to do better. Jerry was the master at this game. At the time, the only required disclosure was the planned compensation, not the actual. There were equity rewards too, but unlike AOL where these were everything, at Time Warner they were not. In addition, corporate officers were eligible for a generous pension. The disclosed compensation looked reasonable.

You can say many things about AOL, but it really was run for the benefit of its shareholders. You cannot say that about Time Warner. To me at least, it sure seemed to be run for the benefit of its management team. The impending culture clash was momentous.

Steve had a major say in the compensation strategy, and it followed AOL principles. The compensation was very generous but heavily weighted toward equity. The Time Warner executives were less than happy with this. This division poisoned the merger from the beginning, but it didn't stop it from happening.

Steve called me during the Christmas holidays to tell me the merger was happening, and he sent the AOL plane to fetch me to allow me to participate. I will always be grateful for that. I flew to New York from Dulles with Colin Powell and Frank Raines, two of the directors who lived in the Washington area. I actually met Frank in 1969 during the Harvard Strike, when he was the chairman of the Student-Faculty Advisory Council, of which I was a member representing graduate students. I only knew Colin from board meetings.

When we got to the board meeting in midtown, the deal was not quite finalized. The directors were given a six-inch-thick binder to review before voting—in an hour! The investment banker refused a fairness opinion unless an additional billion dollars in synergy was identified. Miraculously, within minutes, it was.

Following normal protocol, the seller voted first, and we listened on the conference line as the Time Warner board voted unanimously to approve the transaction. Ted Turner commented that he had not been so happy since the night he first made love to a woman. The executives were happy because with that vote they all vested in their incentive compensation payments, regardless of whether the merger was finalized. This was not at all true for the AOL executives. AOL board approval swiftly followed, also unanimously.

I flew home with Colin and Frank. Colin was kind enough to drive me to my car.

The law on mergers in the United States presents obstacles to any large merger. Except for the press release announcing the merger, no communication between the companies is allowed until legal clearance is received under the Hart-Scott-Rodino Act. This creates a huge void easily filled by rumor and conspiracy theories. In the case of this merger, clearance took a long time. That also meant that the vote by the shareholders to approve the merger had to be postponed, which put extreme pressure on the management teams to hit their numbers. This was purely a stock merger.

In the end, it took over a year before the merger could be closed. I don't know if any deal could survive such a delay. Certainly, this one did not. Time Warner Cable had a complex set of both minority shareholders and franchise agreements to navigate, and they hated the merger. The Xerox phrase "malicious compliance" comes to mind, but I don't know the specifics. Eventually, we were allowed to talk to each other and, eventually, a reorganization of a kind occurred.

THE MERGER

Finally. The merger closed and order was restored, sort of. Steve Case was chairman with some assigned responsibilities, but executives really did not know what he did. In any case, except for me and a few others, everyone else had another boss. Jerry Levin was the CEO, and he acted like he had acted before the merger, like the former CFO he was. He focused on making the numbers—and the promises made to the stock market when the merger was announced were difficult, if not impossible, to meet. He later accepted blame for the failure of the merger.

The businesses reported to co-chief operating officers, Bob Pittman and Dick Parsons. If you ever hear of a business with co-COOs, flee as fast as you can. A position designed to provide operational clarity cannot be shared. It was never clear whether businesses reported to one or to both. It was a mess, but the businesses probably loved it because they could act with little supervision.

Jerry and I got along well, actually. He more than once said to me he had never had a technologist so accomplished or anyone so smart reporting to him. I appreciated the compliments, but I was trying to figure out how to do my job, which really had not changed: figure out the future for a media company. Twenty years later that answer is still emerging.

Jerry and I ended up spending a lot of time together in Europe after 9/11. We had a meeting in Stockholm with the CEO of Sony on the partnership on the AOL broadband box, and return to the US was impossible. We ended up in the UK, and then flew back to Canada when that was possible. By then the rules had been relaxed so some private planes could fly in the US, (though not the one we were in) and one of them picked us up in Montreal and flew us back to New York.

There were two Jerry Levins. When we talked, he was the strategic thinker who created HBO, pushed broadband with Roadrunner, tried to move the magazines online, and, most famously, launched the full-service network in Orlando, giving that test market a taste of what the rest of the country would get a decade or more later. However, as CEO he was the finance geek that focused on getting the numbers better. I never experienced that Jerry.

He explained to me that he basically saw the business as a poker game between the distributors and the content owners. Key to success in his view was being on both sides, so there was always mutually assured destruction. Thus, while they were very different businesses, success in each depended on success in the other. Charter and Xfinity today are closely allied with content assets. He was probably right.

Until you experience it, the difference between these two co-dependent industries would be difficult to believe. Dick Parsons was fond of describing the cable industry as an accident of evolution, in which all remaining Neanderthals ended up working in the same industry. I am not sure he would do that today. The content industry is dominated by fragile, talented egos. Pulling wires through streets or basements is different than writing a story or bringing it to life.

Jerry asked me to write up the cable system of the future, and I did so. We had a great meeting on it, and then I never heard about it again. I understand he gave Joe Collins (former CEO of cable) and Jim Chiddix (who invented modern cable technology) $60 million to build it, but I never heard from them either.

The enmity from the cable company toward AOL was palpable. Jerry did not help by referring to AOL as his national cable company. Every effort at cooperation failed, because cable would not cooperate. A few years later, a friend was in a class at the Tuck School of Business where Glenn Britt, then CEO of cable, was speaking to a class. He was asked about the merger and could not have been more negative in his response.

The whole thesis of the merger was to work with cable and AOL to make a compelling offer to consumers that could then be sold to the other cable companies. Instead, cable did everything in its power to kill AOL—and with support from Dick Parsons came close to doing so. Because AOL was no good with hardware, we secured a deal with Sony for the ABC box that they would manufacture, distribute, and support it. The president of Sony announced it in Las Vegas. Then Dick Parsons killed it silently with a phone call to me, because he said the cable company did not like it. There was no meeting, no discussion even. That was the hardest phone call I ever had to make when I informed Sony of the decision. With that, AOL was doomed to wither away. Profitably but inevitably.

AOL had a serious revenue problem. Broadband was hurting, and growing revenues was hard. Salvation, of sorts, turned up in the form of Level 3, a networking company from Colorado. The largest or second-largest expense for AOL was the inbound modem lines, each of which was an ISDN port on a 5ESS switch. AOL was paying around $125 a month for each. This was billions of dollars in revenue to MCI and Sprint.

When the US deregulated telephones in the United States, it required the local telephone companies to share their local lines with other carriers. Level 3 realized that they could take the inbound modem call at the tandem switch (ahead of the 5ESS), direct it to a bank of DSPs (digital signal processors) from Ascend to convert it to digital, then pass it to a Sun server to transmit it over the network (it worked in reverse as well). Furthermore, under the legal regime in place at the time, the local telephone company had to pay Level 3 $8 a month per line for doing so!

This allowed Level 3 to quote a price of $35 a line (instead of $125), which still afforded them a very healthy margin. AOL had negotiated a deal in which its suppliers had to match the price of any modem supplier that we could sign for at least 100,000 lines. Suddenly the suppliers were faced with a huge loss of revenue and AOL a huge increase in profits.

However, AOL needed revenue growth to please investors. The pressure was put on David Colburn and his team to convert this profit growth into revenue growth. Every quarter had a "go-get" for David of revenue he had to secure with no identified pipeline to do so. He did it quarter after quarter, which is incredible. The last quarter I remember his go-get was $550 million. His deals got inventive, though I never saw the actual agreements.

Beyond helping David and his team, once I was allowed to, I spent much of 2000 just learning about the Time Warner businesses. Bob Pittman wanted some way to offer digital music, and we spent significant energy with Toshiba about an invention they had: a tiny disk drive that could fit into a PCMCIA card (which you could insert into a PC). This could offer a way to distribute digital music in a way that was resistant to piracy. Ultimately, as a Warner Music–only offering it was doomed to fail, so we passed. Toshiba then went to Apple, where it became the foundation of the iPod. The effort did prepare me for the upcoming focus on digital music, however.

MUSIC IN YOUR POCKET

One bright spot in my relationships was Warner Music. Paul Vidich, who functioned as their CTO, and I became very cooperative. There was no question the music industry was challenged. The CD gave them an incredible run. Everyone went out and bought their music library again. The Sony Walkman added portability. Profits flowed. Excess was common. The entire industry was based on identifying and coddling talent.

The CEO of Warner Music, Roger Ames, was (by my estimation) the friendliest division CEO to the merger. He knew music as it was and was struggling to find where it was going. He relied heavily on Paul, who himself was not a technologist. Suddenly, technology had turned from friend to foe.

A major initiative was a format called DVD Audio. While it had DVD in the name, it was separate technology. Listening to music recorded in that format was amazing if you had the right gear to produce it. The music was recorded with more than thirty times as much information per minute as a CD. If you had the master tapes and made a DVD Audio recording, the result was about as close to being there as possible. I still have a few of those disks, and I am amazed when I hear them.

Unfortunately, it took a lot of gear to reproduce the sound properly. Around 2000, the player, amplifier, and speakers were probably in the range of $10,000, and you needed six separate analog cables between the player to the receiver (eventually HDMI would work). You could go much higher. The dream that everyone would buy their library in this new format remained a dream. Very few titles were ever produced. To be fair, there was hope that the car industry would adopt it, but that never happened.

Music at one point was foreground entertainment. I can remember my parents buying a new LP album and then inviting friends over to hear the virgin play. (On vinyl records, every time you play it you lose a little bit of quality.) With a CD, every play is a virgin play. Music was portable, ubiquitous. It became background to life. One study claimed that in only two activities did music remain in the foreground: driving and sex. Arguably, it is still background in those.

When CD-ROM drives were introduced that allowed users to make a CD on a PC, there was panic, but the actual effect was negligible, largely because it was cumbersome and time-consuming. Sales figures suggested that no more than three or four CDs were ever burned per drive sold. The threat to the industry was there, though, as CDs were unprotected and music could be copied. As long as music continued to be sold that way, the threat would just grow. The industry was worried and tried repeatedly to shut it down with legislation.

On June 1, 1999, Shawn Fanning and Sean Parker introduced Napster. Napster allowed "file sharing," which was simply digital piracy. Napster let me expose my music library to others, and they could copy any of my music. I later came to know Sean Parker, and he maintained that his goal was always to make money for the labels. The industry never saw it that way.

The availability of broadband was limited, and Napster was painful over dial-up. However, times were rapidly changing and the industry was in panic. They wanted Congress to protect them, but by not offering any digital music solution as a legal alternative, their pleas were falling on deaf ears.

The industry had a business model that made you buy a whole album on CD to get even a single song. Consumers wanted compilations—custom compilations. There were lots of attempts to offer something, but they simply did not meet customer requirements. Enter Apple, Steve Jobs, and the iPod. Now there was a convenient digital music player that was gaining adoption. Microsoft had a competing technology that met industry security standards, but it was fragile and cumbersome. Stories of users losing all their music in a PC crash meant it would go nowhere.

Roger Ames, urged on by Paul Vidich, went to meet Steve. I was invited as well. Steve did not want any security, though he soon realized it would be to his benefit and agreed to lightweight protection (keeping honest people honest). Eventually agreement was reached on Steve's simple terms: 99 cents per song on unlimited limited devices and five computers. The other labels followed, and history was made. Steve was so thankful to Paul that he made his only attendance at a corporate event for him.

Before this though, we spent months of effort trying to create an alternative that was more to the industry's liking. We did achieve agreement in principle with Sony, but it was much more limited. Sony had gotten bad press (which was well deserved) for embedding malware into its CDs to infect the PC to prevent piracy. A key meeting to push our initiative forward was scheduled for September 11, 2001. Obviously, events intervened.

Shortly thereafter, Paul, myself, and eleven others went to Tokyo for a meeting with Sony. It was a good meeting overall, but on our return flight there was a "misunderstanding" by an air traffic controller in Anchorage, and President Bush signed an order authorizing us to be killed. Two F-16s with Sidewinder missiles arrived to persuade us to land in Brandon, Manitoba. We were taken from the plane at gunpoint, wrapped in carpets, and taken to separate remote locations for questioning. Eventually we were released. Who says corporate life is boring?

Apple included a message in every iPod: *Don't steal music.* That was meant to placate its partners in the music industry, but the whole point of the iPod was to have a portable, large library. No one was likely to buy an iPod to hold fifteen songs. It was a status symbol to have thousands. You could load your existing CDs onto an iPod, and certainly that was done. Apple iTunes software allowed that. However, only the songs in your music library purchased from iTunes were protected. In a university setting, you could expose your library on the network, and anyone on that network could drag and drop your songs into their library. As a result, iTunes almost surely became the principal vector for stealing music. Did Apple know it? Did Steve Jobs know it? They sold a lot of iPods and Macs. In effect, the share of consumer wallets that used to go for music went for computer hardware instead.

The movie industry saw this and tried everything to avoid a similar outcome. VCR tapes could be copied. Everyone knew that, but the quality was low and degraded with repetition: a copy of a copy was better than a copy of a copy of a copy. They knew DVDs were going to pose a risk, so they developed an elaborate scheme to encrypt them. Norwegian Jon cracked it quickly, however. Any scheme that relied upon a secret number known to hundreds of people was doomed to failure.

Nevertheless, the industry tried again with Blu-Ray discs, with a similar but improved scheme. The architects promised the encryption would not be broken for at least a few years. Turned out to be a few months. They were more successful with protecting the output of Blu-Ray (and DVD) players with HDMI, invented by David Lee at Silicon Image.

At this time, streaming was theoretically feasible (at least at low quality), but digital distribution meant digital downloads in general. The capacity of the internet was not there to support high-quality streaming. Downloads took minutes, even hours. Clever software was developed to speed this up, which the industry fought. Portals to sell digital movies were created, but they never gained volume.

I learned a lot about the movie business from Warren Lieberfarb, who was considered the father of the DVD. We got along, even though he was another hater of the merger. The DVD was more than the movie content. Picking it out was often a family adventure, maybe even a weekly one. The cases mattered a lot for this reason, just as book covers matter so much. Walmart exploited this by selling DVDs below cost to get families into the store. Warren told me once that more than half of all DVDs were sold through Walmart. He claimed more than 25 percent of DVDs were never watched: people just wanted to "own" their favorite film. A film might bomb at the box office but sell incredibly well on DVD. *Pearl Harbor* did that. The reverse was also true.

The movie industry lives off of *windows*. Movies are released through successive windows. First is box office, then pay-per-view, then more general pay-per-view, then pay television, then . . . The whole goal is to capture as much value as possible. An economist would call this "scooping out the demand curve." Piracy is an existential threat to this model.

In addition, movie revenue is affected by two interrelated but separate factors: the number of people who see it and the number of times they see it. *Titanic* was a megahit because lots of people saw it *and* most people saw it more than once, many times more than once.

Text messaging and social media threatened the first window. Early viewers could tank a movie at the box office even by time zones. East Coast viewer comments changed the box office results on the West Coast. Dating apps also changed the market. In the years after World War II, more than half of all Americans would see a movie at a theater on the weekend. That erosion continues, as did the nostalgia.

I gained great respect for how hard the industry actually was. I think I contributed a lot in conversations, and I had some good relationships. However, they were and are a very independent group.

The copy protection focus shifted to television and the digital video recorder. There is some karma in this, because the team that built TiVo was the team that had built much of the full-service network experiment in Orlando done by Time Warner Cable. At the time, this was a real technological feat, but as technology improved it became easier and easier. Cable did offer pay-per-view movies, but the Hollywood blockbusters were cover for the adult entertainment, which was extremely profitable. The experience was not great, and the quality was marginal. DVRs changed everything.

Up to a third of all ads on TV were ads for TV. Programming was made to keep you from changing channels. Ads were targeted by time and content. All of that was challenged by DVRs, which allowed you to "time shift." You could watch a show or movie when you wanted. Moreover, you could easily skip commercials. Again, technology was not a friend because the storage possibilities just kept getting larger.

CONSTANT CONTENT

In classic AOL fashion, a corporate team was formed to look at the future of television. Jeff Bewkes, the CEO of HBO, presented it to the board, but he did not participate in developing the report. This was no surprise—he was the most ardent opponent of the merger and wore it on his sleeve. He was a firm believer that if you had the content, you were in control of your destiny. Distribution was for lesser mortals.

I met with all the CEOs in my role as CTO. My meeting with Jeff was interesting. He said he hated me less than the other AOL people, because I did not make money on the merger. I thought it a funny way to start a conversation, especially since he did. He complained bitterly to me about having his compensation changed from cash (I think he was earning around $15 million a year) to stock.

Our meeting was then interrupted by a call from Tom Hanks asking for a partnership around *Band of Brothers*. Jeff was very crisp in our meeting. He said his biggest competitive advantage was that he could say "fuck." Indeed, the president of NBC ran full-page ads asking for equality on that subject. I learned a lot in the meeting. It was clear HBO was going to be a reluctant partner at best to any of the strategic plans we had.

Jeff was very good at what he did. When he took over HBO, he made a bold decision. He decided that the key to success was original content and the fear of missing out. He gave 90 percent of his original programming budget to David Chase and told him to build a compelling show. He did. *The Sopranos*.

The rest of his programming lineup he filled with cheap shows, many about sex. One was a documentary on the Nevada brothel the Bunny Ranch. They filmed the bargaining conversation between client and prostitute for sixty-three clients. When the clients left, they were given a choice to destroy that video or sign a waiver to have it possibly used in the show. The producers expected maybe one in three would sign the waiver. Sixty-one of the sixty-three did. The clients covered a wide spectrum, and the show was a success. Someone then realized that in New York state, if you are committing an illegal act, you have no expectation of privacy. Thus they shifted future shows to New York and did not need to ask for waivers. People were apparently surprised to find themselves on HBO.

One of the shows that HBO had at the time was a special with Robin Williams. Jeff told me that his major contribution that year had been in reversing the order of the final two segments. You can watch the show to judge for yourself. The close of the show was a live performance on Broadway. That same day there was a meeting of the AOL Time Warner board of directors, and at the end of the meeting there was a lot of chatter about the event. The chatter became awkward when people realized one person did not have an invitation: Steve Case, the chairman of the board. One was found, but the seat next to him was empty, making him look isolated. People were sure it was intentional, although I suspect it was simply that they only had tickets in pairs. Needless to say, I was never invited.

HBO was a subscription service, but it had no idea who its subscribers were. The subscription agreement was with the MSOs, Multiple System Operators, primarily the cable companies. After Congress passed a law requiring it, DirecTV (and other satellite operators) was also granted the right to carry HBO. On top of that, a large percentage of HBO subscribers did not receive a bill for it, but instead got it as a promotion from the MSO.

HBO was conceived by Jerry Levin as a means of monetizing the Warner Brothers film library, and that library still made up a lot of the viewing hours HBO offered. Over time, though, original productions beginning with *The Sopranos* began to dominate the brand promise. At the beginning of HBO, staffers there told me they thought the number one reason people bought HBO was the "mother-in-law" factor: the fear of not being able to find something to watch for a family gathering. (Yes, once upon a time, people gathered in a room and watched a television show together, however quaint that may seem today.) Under Jeff it was a very successful and profitable business.

The content owners had an opportunity with the MSOs that they probably never understood, but which would have potentially changed the industry's trajectory. Cable Labs, the cooperative that did technology research and development for the industry, had adopted Java as a technology. Thus, it was possible that if you wanted to watch content on your DVR from a particular network, you could have required that it be done through an interface the network owner provided in Java. I explained this to Bob Kimmitt, my colleague and head of public policy for the company, and he joined me in trying to get Warner Broadcasting to push for it. The meeting was polite, but it was clear it was never going to happen.

THE LONG GOODBYE

AOL remained a major area of focus for me. Barry Schuler was named CEO when the merger closed, and I went to congratulate him. For the second time in my career, he thanked me but assured me he would be fired within a year. The budget requirements for AOL in the annual plan were simply unattainable, and he was right. I shared many rides to and from New York with David Colburn and learned how right he was. As a result, he certainly lacked enthusiasm for his role.

After Barry Schuler left, Bob Pittman stepped down as co-COO of AOL Time Warner and returned as CEO of AOL. He was sure he could quickly fix the revenue problem. He was wrong, and that may tell you something about why AOL was in trouble. Bob invented online advertising, and he sold the first deals himself. No one had any idea what to charge for these ads, and Bob struck good deals. By the time he returned, the industry had a much lower price point. And there was the broadband issue.

He was replaced by Jon Miller, whom I had not met. We developed a good rapport. In our first meeting, he asked me a great question, "What advice would you give me that no one else would?" I answered that he should gather the top 500 people in a room and then randomly select half to leave. I thought AOL had clogged arteries and would be more successful with fewer employees. He later told a reporter it was the piece of advice he had gotten in his career that he most regretted not following.

We had an incredibly consequential meeting early on, but for Google not AOL, though it wasn't bad for AOL. Jon and I visited Google at their early campus in Mountain View, buildings which had once been Sun buildings. The waiting room had a live feed of searches being run, although the public one had been filtered already as so many searches were definitely NSFW. AOL had to choose a new search vendor, and I thought Google was the best possible choice. They offered an incredible economic deal to make it easy. Eric Schmidt later told me this was the deal that tipped the scales for Google. Sergei Brin was incredibly good in selling to Jon. AOL also won, because it had the best search.

We tried other ideas to make AOL, the service, better. One was an early idea like DropBox. Most downloaded files were then sent on to others, and transmitting them through the narrow pipe of dial-up both ways was very time-consuming. We looked at caching them at AOL to avoid that. We also looked at making the AOL session traffic encrypted (SSL), because that would allow us to put sensitive information on the home screen. We looked at adding a phone number to every AOL account. We did gain integration between AOL Instant Messenger and text messaging, which was magical: you turned up in my buddy list when you turned on your cell phone. Few got that feature though. AIM, by then run by Chamath Palihapitiya, was becoming more and more the mainstay of loyalty to AOL.

Matt Korn had worked for years to secure settlement-free peering for AOL. Translated this meant free internet access. AOL was a peer to the tier 1 network operators, so it did not have to pay anyone for sending or receiving internet access. This was a huge win. Corporate did not see it that way, so it was abandoned. That in general was the problem. Corporate never understood AOL once it became managed by former Time Warner executives. The ideas to make the service itself better just never got done. Deprecation was the order of the day.

. I was reporting to Jeff Bewkes once Steve Case was forced out, though I suspected my time was limited. Dick Parsons really did not care much for technology. Once during a strategy workshop, David Eun, then a vice president in the strategy group, was presenting all the interactions with Microsoft. Dick and Jeff were both in attendance. Dick fell asleep. David did not know what to do. Jeff told him that it did not matter and to keep presenting. He was probably right.

At a meeting in December, Dick asked me to update him, and a meeting was set up. He began the meeting with "these meetings are always hard." Picking up on the theme, I answered that I had an employment contract. He was shocked. He said I never signed the one corporate had sent me, and I said he was correct because I had more favorable terms already. He asked if I would send him the contract, and I said yes. And that was that. To his credit, he honored it to the letter. They also did not have the intellectual property agreement and never asked for it, though the final separation agreement was awkward as they kept referring to it. They should have, because they did later sell the patents on which I was the listed inventor to Microsoft. I am surprised Microsoft due diligence did not ask for it.

His next meeting was Jon Miller, who was laying out his strategy for AOL, and he began by saying how reliant he was going to be on me. Dick told him that I was gone, and Jon asked if he could rehire me. This annoyed everyone. At first it was approved only if I agreed to reduce my severance payments dollar for dollar (i.e., work for free). Eventually, we reached agreement for one year, and when Jon wanted to renew it, he was denied. I had to leave my corporate boards at Dick's direction. It was corporate policy, but I was told it was only enforced against me. The culture was poisoned against AOL and its people.

Content was king at Time Warner and again at AOL Time Warner, and for reasons I still find hard to fathom, that meant technology could not be important. It is not a logical choice; a culture simply cannot tolerate more than one group of priests. Managing technology in media remains challenging for this reason.

I did chair a technology council of all the CTOs, and I believe the meetings actually were useful, more because we brought people together. We talked about new developments and challenges. Dick loved that we met.

The other major thing I remember is that I got an approach from Microsoft about settling the antitrust suit AOL had filed. I am not sure why me, but the CTO was a logical place to start. It was a deniable approach from a dealmaker, not a senior executive. Steve Ballmer was then CEO of Microsoft and is a former student of mine. He once told a reporter I was the only person he talked to who sued him three times for antitrust and won all three. Steve maybe suggested me. Anyway, once I duly reported the approach, I was shoved out of the way, and Jeff Bewkes took charge. A settlement was reached for $750 million, and I would guess Microsoft was pleased with that outcome.

Jerry Levin was always a cable guy at heart, and he saw dominating that industry as *the* strategic play. Just as he had in negotiating with Steve over the AOL merger, Jerry negotiated a deal with AT&T to merge their respective cable assets into a new company in which AOL Time Warner would hold just over 40 percent of the stock. When he heard of it, Mike Kelly, the chief financial officer, said they needed to talk to the board of directors.

That meeting did not go well, and Jerry was forced out of his job. Steve called me and felt this was going to mean success for the merger. Steve is such a nice person, he never instinctively understood how viciously the power game was played at Time Warner. Dick Parsons did. Steve thought the outcome was going to be Dick reporting to him as executive chairman, but that did not happen. I helped Steve write his email contributions to the strategy discussion that ensued, but the governance committee picked Dick. When Dolf DiBasio, whom Dick hired as head of strategy, asked Dick for his input on strategy, he said Dick told him it was simple, "Execute."

Thus ended my tenure at AOL Time Warner, although I was kept on for another year advising AOL. The name was soon changed back to just Time Warner, and the narrative is always about how Time Warner made a mistake in buying AOL. That is incorrect. AOL bought Time Warner, but that ruins the narrative. Was there a strategy? Yes. Could it have worked? Yes. Why did it fail? Bewkes claimed the people cooperated well but it was simply a flawed idea. He saw a different enactment than I did. In 2002, my Castle Lecture at West Point was on why good leaders make horrible technology decisions. It is a complicated question, but my time at AOL Time Warner was a master class in it.

CHAPTER 10

RUCKUS NETWORK (2004–2006)

FTER AOL TIME WARNER, I LOOKED AT A FEW SIMILAR COR-PORATE JOBS, BUT TO BE HONEST MY HEART WAS NOT IN IT. I had multiple little companies where I was a board member or advisor, and I was a strategic advisor to AOL. I was pretty busy, though the compensation rate was low.

Vince Han and David Galper came to sell me on becoming CEO of Ruckus Network, a startup they had founded. The idea looked compelling: the music industry was actively filing lawsuits against college students for music theft—one college student was required to pay damages of over one billion dollars (i.e., file bankruptcy). Ruckus proposed to provide free music to university students, paid for by the university. On the surface, it looked great.

The idea actually originated with Scott Tobin, a partner at Battery Ventures, and he was sponsoring Vince and David. It was already moving forward in Boston with a technology team and a business development manager, Charlie Moore.

A deal had been struck for limited access to movies, and the music deals were in progress. We agreed on funding and on relocating to Northern Virginia. All seemed good.

Things went smoothly at first. I hired Nancy Hauge as head of human resources and Doug Wallace as CFO. We became good friends, and they both tried their best to drive success. We opted for a young team to match the market and hired some real talent. Art Bilger joined as an investor, and he suggested Farrell Reynolds as head of sales. A great hire. We were rocking.

Or so I thought. The technology team started missing deadlines. The product was incomplete and unusable. Early on, Scott Tobin had told Larry Cheng to go hire a team and he did so. They were an enterprise software team using heavy-duty and inappropriate tools to build a consumer product. I later learned that at least some planned to leave to work for someone else and needed someone else to pay them in the interim.

Charlie Moore took his orders from Scott, not me. He knew his next job was likely to come through Scott and placed his loyalty there. Scott used to go visit the technology team and Charlie in Boston and give them direction, without telling me. The result was we immediately had a we/they problem between Boston and Virginia that we could never solve.

There were four huge surprises, that maybe should not have been. First, we thought the music industry would be our friends, as we were trying to stop music piracy. While they did make some accommodations, we were just another customer charged standard prices, which were too high for the market. When I complained, they pointed to their antitrust consent decree for cover. We did get discounts, but had to pay content fees.

Second, we thought universities cared about music theft. They did, but as the vice president of student affairs at American University told me, it was tenth on her priority list after alcohol abuse in the first six places and sexual abuse in the next three. They legally had to care, but stealing music was not something they really cared about.

Third, we bet on Microsoft technology for copy protection that the music industry would accept. I tried to get a deal with Apple, but got back a 2 a.m. email from Steve Jobs saying people wanted to own not rent music. The Microsoft technology met the requirements of the music industry, but it was just too complicated and fragile. There were also no good portable players to match Apple.

Fourth, we did not realize our major competitor was going to be Apple making free music widely available in universities. Their public stance was "Don't steal music!" but the most effective tools for music theft ever invented were the initial versions of Apple iTunes. Students on university networks could just drag and drop libraries from others into their libraries and install on their iPods, which were the new rage as we were trying to launch.

We got a few deals, but customer success stories were few and far between. The product was really not that good. We had the major music sources and ten rotating movies. Our original supplier of movies, Swank, pulled our deal at the last minute, and we survived on a deal with Warner Brothers we had only because I knew the CEO from Time Warner. The player was cumbersome, and the selection of devices was mediocre. Some young males were apparently successful at meeting young women by installing Ruckus on their computers, but that was not sustainable.

Noah Szubski worked in marketing, and he was and is a genius at online marketing. He realized the power of the Facebook feed before Facebook did. I took some staff to dinner on a Thursday night and learned he had made a post with two phony accounts saying that if they became the most popular group on Facebook, his girlfriend would give him a threesome.

During dinner, excitement started to build as the number in the group grew by tens of thousands. By early Friday afternoon, Noah had hundreds of thousands joining. A recurrent question in the post was what the fans would get. Responding to that, Noah said that if the group reached 600,000, he would post video. Dustin Moskowitz pulled the plug Tuesday afternoon at about 450,000. Noah had decided it had gone too far when *Time* magazine called for an interview. A few months later, I brought Noah to a dinner in Oakland with Dustin, Peter Thiel, Mark Zuckerberg, and some others. It was just a marketing prank, but it proved how viral the feed could be. David Kirkpatrick included this incident without names in his seminal book on Facebook.

Things got ugly at Ruckus eventually. We needed a reset, but for that we needed money. I attracted interest, but Scott Tobin was adamant that there could be no down round. He had overplayed Ruckus to his limited partners as a huge potential success, and that was critical to his firm. The Boston team, even under new management, remained aloof and almost insubordinate. Instead of spending my time on the business, I was constantly trying to raise money.

The four surprises probably made success impossible. Our last swing was to make Ruckus ad-supported. Christian Celic, who worked for Farrell, did a presentation on how we could do this profitably. It turned out to be wrong. Scott made Farrell CEO and me chairman. Soon I was gone completely, and a new CEO was hired. But the four surprises were still there. I never learned how it ended. I still ask myself what I could have done differently.

CHAPTER 11

THE ADVISOR: NASPERS, OPERA, AND DMGT (1999–2021)

NASPERS

AT SUN I SPONSORED A STRATEGIC DEAL WITH THOMSON CON-
SUMER ELECTRONICS ON SET-TOP BOXES. This venture eventually evolved into Open TV, which went public during
the DotCom boom in November 1999 with a peak value over
$1 billion. It evolved into a partnership with Myriad Inter-
national Holdings, Ltd., which in turn was the internet arm
of Naspers, a South African corporation. I had left Sun by
then and am not sure what Sun finally realized from its 20
percent stake.

During apartheid in South Africa, its companies were
global pariahs and so had to become self-sufficient. Naspers
owned Multichoice, which was the major satellite television
provider to Africa. The technology was homegrown because
it had to be. They needed a new, more powerful operating

system for their set-top boxes, and Open TV was their path. Naspers also owned Irdeto, which provided content security.

Out of this relationship grew a friendship with Naspers that lasted fifteen years. Koos Bekker, its CEO, is probably the best CEO I have met in my career. When we met, Naspers had a market capitalization of $400 million, if I remember correctly. At its peak it reached $50 billion. He did this with a core team of less than twenty people, though they could call on their newspaper company for administrative support. I worked closely throughout with his effective COO, Cobus Stofberg. Because of the historic apartheid restrictions, the businesses outside of South Africa were in a separate company, Myriad International Holdings, in the Netherlands. Today MIH is Proteus, which is in a complicated cross-ownership with Naspers. Cobus was the CEO of MIH. The boards were almost the same. Until Time Warner forced me off, I was a director of MIH for a while.

Koos had a simple business strategy. Find an internet business that worked well in the US and bring it to less-developed markets. He would buy around 80 percent of the local company and insist on control of the checkbook by bringing in a CFO. He was remarkably successful in keeping the local CEOs in place. They stayed and were loyal. These companies were managed through conference calls and twice-yearly operations reviews. These were very thorough but polite. Naspers management asked questions. They did not give answers. However, if you did not answer them promptly, you might be looking for a job. He was a leader who understood how to lead.

Key to that leadership were two annual conferences held each year in different locations all over the world. One was for CEOs and the other was on internet strategy. My role was to give a talk at one or both, synthesizing what was happening in the rest of the world. In between, I did give advice when asked, and I mingled with their people. The quality was so high. Americans would have dismissed them for their pedigree in general, but Koos certainly knew how to pick the wheat from the chaff, and how to manage through questions. At the conferences he was an active participant, constantly asking questions and emphasizing learning.

On my sixty-fifth birthday, I was in one such meeting in Istanbul in the Hagia Irene in the Topkapi Palace (closed to the public, but somehow Naspers got around these restrictions). It has the best natural acoustics of any building in Europe. Naspers had hired Benjamin Zander, conductor of the Boston Philharmonic Orchestra in Boston, as their speaker. He had a gimmick he used, which was to sing "Happy Birthday" to someone. Koos knew it was my birthday, and soon I was standing on a chair in front of the crowd. Zander asked them all to sing, but it was weak. He then organized them and conducted the next rendition. It was one of the most moving moments of my life.

I got involved early on when they looked at investing in a Chinese internet business. It was located in a walkup on the second floor off a street where street merchants would sell you pirated copies of almost any DVD. It reminded me of Facebook when they were on Emerson Street in Palo Alto. The investment was messy because of the $35 million ask—$25 million was going to go to the five founders ($5 million each) and only $10 million into the company. US venture capital firms passed. Koos took it. He got 35 percent of Tencent for $35 million.

Its peak market capitalization reached over $2 trillion.

During the first financial review, I was invited to a meeting where Tencent presented their idea to go into gaming, branching out from their messaging business. It was approved, obviously. Tencent had a privileged position in China. There are fifty-three provinces with four cellular networks in each. It is not permitted to send a text message across networks. However, you can use QQ messaging from Tencent to do so. This conveniently means Tencent has all the messaging traffic, and the PLA (People's Liberation Army) has floors of censors co-located. I once got off on the wrong floor, but immediately I knew it was a mistake.

My last time at Tencent, President Hui of the People's Republic of China visited unannounced. He spent time with Pony Ma, founder and CEO, and then came down to declare China needed more people like Pony, a billionaire living in Hong Kong. In every interaction I had with Pony, I was impressed. He had the consumer instincts of Steve Case and the software ability of Mark Zuckerberg combined with an uncanny ability to navigate Chinese politics. Tencent outgrew me, but I value the time I spent with them and with David Wallerstein, who is still their chief explorations officer. Naspers had an honored position in China because they helped the government when no one else did. I am not sure any other non-Chinese company would be allowed to own so much of such an important company.

My first visit to China with Naspers was supposed to be at the Sheraton Hotel, which had just opened. However, hints were dropped that it was too ostentatious, so we were rerouted to the Holiday Inn Lido, the first foreign hotel in

China. Threadbare is one description. Prostitutes waited in the lobby to jump into the elevator at the last minute if you were male and alone. We survived.

My last meeting was in South Africa. Surveying the enormous lunch buffet, I asked the conference coordinator how many diets she had to support. Fifty-three was her answer. I know of no other company that has created such a powerful cooperative culture across so many diverse countries. This is a true tribute to Koos. He also showed the world the right way to exit. He hired a CEO and then got out of his way, though he remains chair. I will always cherish the time I spent with him, Cobus, and the people of Naspers.

OPERA (2006-2007)

At Sun, we had needed a browser, and I attempted to acquire Opera Software, in Oslo, Norway. I was in Europe on other business and went to meet them on a holiday. Because it was a holiday, there was no one at immigration, so I had a big problem when attempting to leave without an inbound entry stamp. Norway is pretty strict on these things.

Gier Isovay, the founder, was one of those truly brilliant programmers; tragically, he died young. In terms of size, the Opera browser was tiny. Less than 10 percent the size of Mozilla, but just as functional if not more so. Just brilliant code. I was the executive who put Mozilla into open source from Netscape, so there was some irony in this. Gier and I had a good dinner, and I later made an offer, which they declined. It was primarily in Sun stock. If they had taken that offer they would have made more money than they did in the end going public.

Anyway, through these discussions I got to know Jon von

Tetzchner, the CEO and co-founder. Over a dinner near my house, he asked if I would consider joining the board. There were some interviews, and in 2006 I was added to the board. Again, I was a victim of not doing enough due diligence.

Opera basically survived as a reseller of Google search. It was wonderful if you were on a dial-up or another weak connection, so it was very popular in Russia where network connections were weak. It was fast and small and did everything you needed it to do. There was a dedicated community of users.

I showed up for my first board meeting, and Nils Foldal, the chair on the nominations committee, moved to fire Jon. This was all news to me. I asked who was going to replace him, and Nils was unsure. I counseled against doing anything so precipitously, and we did not fire him.

Norwegian corporate governance has its oddities. The board had three (later four) members elected by the employees. The shareholders had five members, at least 40 percent of whom had to be women. To maintain board independence, there was a separate nominations committee that nominated board members and recommended their compensation. The members of that committee were separately elected by the shareholders. Importantly, they did not have fiduciary duty to the company like the directors. The annual accounts had to be approved at an in-person meeting in Oslo and signed by the chairman. There were others, but these were the major differences—except for one.

Norway followed German law; the CEO was expected to act in the interests of all stakeholders and could be dismissed only for cause. He or she could challenge a dismissal in court, but was not permitted to be a director of the company. This creates a very interesting dynamic.

I was clearly the director with the most knowledge and experience. No other shareholder director was in technology, and the employee directors were pretty focused on writing software and not general business. After the first year, I became chairman. Nils claimed the power of the nominations committee to pick the chairman, but while this could be true in a private company, in a public company the board elected the chairman after the annual meeting.

I am used to CEOs carefully managing what the board knows, but Jon took it to another level. Google offered to adopt Opera as the basis for what became Chrome, and Jon turned them down without even telling the board about the possibility.

Jon was committed to a belief in what he called Opera Unite. Opera Unite was a brilliant idea, and in some other universe could have been an incredible success. Unfortunately, not in the universe in which we live. His idea was to turn every instance of Opera into a web server so you could easily host from your computer. It worked really well. There were just not many interested customers. The biggest issue is that almost all broadband networks in the world aren't symmetric: outbound bandwidth is less than inbound, often much less. Opera Unite is ill-suited for that. Moreover, most people do not like leaving their personal computers on constantly. To give Jon the credit he is due, the basic need he was meeting is the compulsion to share. Facebook did that better.

Two engineers did a rogue project that became Opera Mini. This was a huge commercial success, but it was never a formal company strategy. It was almost falling off a log for Opera. Because it was optimized for dial-up networks, when you visited a page, it saved it in a highly compressed form so you could go back to it without reloading. Cell phones and cell phone bandwidth at the time were both limited. The Opera Mini app on your phone talked to an instance of Opera on a server in Iceland, which fetched the page, compressed it, and sent it back to you. This was a much better user experience. Iceland had great connectivity from its NATO ties and was midway between the US and Europe. The data center was a former bunker. Air conditioning was opening the window. The Opera team did a great job in scaling up the operation quickly.

Most web pages in the beginning of the internet were a single request, but modern web pages (even a decade ago) were tens and even hundreds of requests for a single page; what looks like a page to you is actually a complex program with multiple requests for data. Doing these on the server with a high-speed connection and having only one transmission to the phone was just much better. Opera was optimized to run in a multi-user environment and to compress web pages, so there was no basic engineering needed to support it. We soon had hundreds of servers in Iceland. Searches went to Google, which paid us.

Opera Mini was free, but there was no app store yet, so the carriers wanted to preinstall it. Handset control was important then: the ability to dictate what software was on the phone. We could charge 50 euro cents per phone for something we gave away for this privilege, and business boomed.

Opera Mini created a problem in China, because it evaded

the Great Firewall. Our young manager there got a call one day saying he was going to get some visitors. Six vice ministers arrived. He was nervous. Vice ministers are powerful people and six is a lot. Having them come to see you on official business is not something you wish for. No orders were given, but a suggestion was made that if Opera Mini worked normally for foreign cell phones but went through the Great Firewall for Chinese phones, people would be very happy. We followed their suggestion.

Opera Mini was popular in China because we had a deal with the largest retailer of cell phones in China. I will always remember my dinner with their CEO. I doubt I have ever met a more entrepreneurial entrepreneur. At that time, cell carriers were not allowed to sell hardware, so the resellers had handset control, not the carrier. That deal meant Opera Mini was on most of the cell phones sold in China. Eventually Chinese investors were the buyers of the browser business.

I waited in line in 2007 in Palo Alto to get the first iPhone to bring to my Opera board meeting. As you would expect, the general reaction at Opera was skepticism that it would ever succeed. Incumbents almost always discount new competition. I realized we needed a new horse to ride.

We got it in 2010 when David Widen, whom I knew from AOL, called me from Khosla Ventures to see if we would be interested in acquiring Admarvel, a mobile phone advertising company, for $8 million. Led by Mahi de Silva, Admarvel had a great team, but no one was willing to fund the next round. It was a hard sell to the management team, but eventually I prevailed. Opera eventually sold it for $1.4 billion. It was a good deal, and mobile advertising became the mainstay of the business. Opera eventually sold the browser business and rebranded as Otello Corporation.

Relationships between Jon and the board became contentious. Nils was no longer on the board, but as chairman of the nominations committee he acted as if he was the controlling shareholder. He represented the largest shareholder, but they were not controlling, and under Norwegian law we had to consider all stakeholders. He was certainly agitating, but Jon was obstinate.

I flew to California to meet Jon for dinner at Il Fornaio in Burlingame. I advised him that he was going to be fired if he did not do at least one of three things, all of which I thought were easy. I don't remember the details, but I remember his emphatic rejection. When I walked into the board meeting, he took me aside and warned me I was going to lose. The vote was 8–0. Sad day for all concerned really. We offered him a role as strategic advisor, but he soon left in anger. Lars Boilesen, his successor, has done a good job in navigating the company through many changes.

I did learn how different Europe is from the United States. We were in a board meeting, and suddenly Jon had to leave for a call. It was the competition commissioner from the European Union calling. She asked Jon if Opera could file an antitrust complaint against Microsoft before 5 p.m. that day. She assured Jon we would win, as she was the judge. Eventually, Opera got a $12.5 million payment from an unidentified multinational corporation.

I loved this company and enjoyed the people, but even though I have flown twelve million miles in the last forty years, travel to Oslo was just too often and arduous. There were no nonstop flights then, and hospitality is not the Norwegian habit. I was making eight trips a year. For the annual accounts, I would show up for ten minutes and sign, but that was the law.

On the other side, Norwegian culture says that board service is an honor and the pay should be minimal. Options had limited terms, so they were not worth that much. Nils controlled compensation, and he was cheap with it. He was also calling me multiple times a week with suggestions on what I needed to make management do. After a very successful financial year, I decided it was time to go. I was surprised by the warmth of my fellow board members at the farewell. They were good people doing their best for the company. If I made any good personnel decision in my career, it was backing Lars for CEO.

DAILY MAIL AND GENERAL TRUST (2010–2021)

The Daily Mail and General Trust is the parent company of the London *Daily Mail*, one of the top daily newspapers in the United Kingdom and one of the largest English-language websites in the world. It is credited with enormous political influence. It was and is a conservative newspaper with conservative views.

When I started advising them, the weekday paper sold over one million copies daily at the newsstand. The Saturday paper sold more (it included the weekly TV guide), and the Sunday sister publication, the *Mail on Sunday*, which has a separate editorial team, sold almost as many. The newspapers historically were very profitable.

DMGT today is a privately-held corporation in London, owned by family trusts of the founders and represented by

Viscount (Jonathan) Rothermere, the chairman of the board of directors. He is a true gentleman who taught me much about the difference between viewing things as an owner instead of as an employee. He takes his heritage and his duty very seriously.

Until the end of 2022, DMGT was a public company listed on the London Stock Exchange. While Lord Rothermere was an active executive chairman, he was not the CEO. Since he represents the controlling shareholders, he obviously has a strong voice in any decision. The day-to-day running of the corporation was the responsibility of the CEO, although Jonathan was more active in running the newspaper.

Jonathan's father had started to diversify the business. Jonathan continued the diversification when he became chairman at age twenty-nine after the death of his father. The diversification once included taxi cabs and pizza shops, but by the time I joined, there was just an extensive collection of business-to-business information companies.

The largest and first of these was Euromoney, which was a spinout from DMGT. Euromoney was publicly traded even though DMGT owned 67 percent of its shares and reported consolidated financials, because there was a contract between the two companies in which DMGT agreed to limit its control. It was an ambiguous situation, but it largely worked, in part because of a long-standing relationship with the founder. Euromoney, in turn, was a collection of businesses very loosely coupled to the center.

The third major piece of the company was Risk Management Solutions, headquartered in California. RMS had and has an enviable franchise as the leading supplier of catastrophe models, quantifying by location potential damage from hurricanes, earthquakes, floods, wildfires, and other natural hazards. Their customers were insurers, reinsurers, and insurance brokers.

As an insurance provider, you are expected to set aside reserves to cover underwriting risks, and by the nature of the business, the size of these reserves determines your profitability. Regulators and accountants want evidence that the reserves are properly sized, and RMS became the standard by which that was done. This is an enviable position to have, and RMS had an enviable history of both growth and profitability. While there was a board of directors of DMGT executives and some independent members, RMS was dominated by its CEO, who had founded the company out of Stanford with his father.

Then there were the other business-to-business companies, some recently acquired but some not. The DMGT promise to its shareholders was to provide a growing stream of cash dividend payments by growing operating profits. This was the bottom line. Buying small startup companies within this mantra was never going to be easy.

DMGT solved this as best they could by promising light-touch management and providing relatively large and generous cash incentives (earnouts) to the founders to induce them to sell. These were relatively small companies with revenues in the tens of millions of dollars, all managed by an executive reporting to the DMGT CEO. Each company had its own board and board meetings and its own culture.

Finally, there was a specialized events business that largely operated large exhibitions in the Middle East and interacted little with the rest of the corporation.

This was a fascinating, diverse portfolio, and managing such a portfolio will always be challenging. The timeframe of the DMGT shareholders is very long-term. The startup founders inherently looked at their earnout period. This was life, but it was a deep conflict of interest. However, that was not obvious, and I was a believer too.

Except for the events business, information technology was moving from being a support service to a strategic one. None of the businesses saw themselves as technology-driven, even though technology was increasingly critical to their operations and survival. Jonathan saw the trend and wanted to hire a chief technology officer, but his management team objected (I understand), so he decided to hire a consultant.

John Cummins is a legendary adviser to senior management teams. I first met him at Naspers. I did not appreciate his skill until a decade later. We were planning to have dinner in London the next Friday, and I called him on Sunday to set the plans. I asked him what he was doing, and he said he was being the board assassin for a public company. I asked for clarification, and he said he was writing the board a report that the board was going to use to fire the CEO. At our Friday dinner, he received two text messages close to each other. The first, from the lead director, said, "Thank you. A 22-caliber round right between the eyes. Clean kill." The second from the newly terminated CEO said, "Thank you. I could not have gotten through this without your help." He is good. Very good.

Anyway, he has a long-standing relationship with Jonathan, whom he separately had advised to hire a technology consultant. John recommended me, and one day at RMS I met Joe McCollum, the DMGT head of human resources, who John had also recommended to Jonathan. After many more interviews, Martin Morgan, the CEO, hired me for an initial assignment. I thought it was on information technology, but, in retrospect, it was on management alignment. I wish I'd understood that then.

One of the best things I did at Sun was hold an annual system adequacy review with each business. The idea came from Michaele James, and it worked very well, though it annoyed my colleagues. I followed the same general theme now at DMGT. We asked each business to inventory the systems on which they depended and to state whether they were adequate for current and future business requirements. If they weren't, what were they going to do about it?

DMGT had very good, well-meaning people, and compliance was excellent. The results were sobering. *Hodgepodge* would be an understatement. Every system was bespoke. Many systems were utterly outdated. RMS had by far the best team and the most rigorous technology management. Euromoney was the one most in need of help. The industry phrase for systems that need work is *technology debt*. DMGT had a lot of it, but so do most companies.

Any company with cash incentive programs, in my experience, ends up with a lot of technology debt. The reason is simple: technology maintenance can almost always be postponed, and the costs of doing so are not very visible. Managers achieve their bonuses by delaying maintenance. DMGT was by no means unusual.

Large earnouts are generally successful at generating short-term business success. However, they discourage management from investing in the subsequent years, and they mask the compensation requirement needed once the earnout ends. People see cash as cash, and putting different labels on it is irrelevant. So if the founders are effectively taking home $2 million or $3 million per year during the earnout period, they are not staying around for 25–35 percent of that. So they leave. The successors hired at lower compensation rates are not as good, so the business struggles.

Thus, the earnouts are effective at enabling acquisitions but make long-term success more difficult to achieve. A side effect is that the accounting profits are biased upwards because the direct compensation effectively could be lower because of the earnouts. Computing this was very judgmental. The challenges with LTIPs and earnouts are not specific to DMGT. They were issues at Naspers. Indeed, at every company. They go with the territory.

Anyway, we collected the results, and I reported them to a management team meeting at a hotel in London. I knew everyone a little but beyond Martin Morgan and Joe McCollum not very much. Jonathan the least. He put me on the spot immediately—a skill he has mastered. He asked me what to do.

By then I had learned that the company was devoted to light-touch management, so I tempered my reply accordingly. I suggested creating four "utilities," each reporting to its own board composed of company CEOs. One would do mobile software, one data center operations, one data analysis, and one databases. The goal was to create talent magnets, centers of excellence, and shared efficiency. It was not a bad answer theoretically, but from the body language (though not the words) it was clear immediately that it was not going to happen. This is the reason technology debt persists so long—there is no easy way to remediate it.

I don't know today if I should have answered differently. It is not my nature to not try to answer a question such as his to the best of my ability. But I was new to the company and its politics and was certainly pushing the limits of what an advisor should do. On the other hand, I was doing what I thought I was being paid to do.

I tried hard to sell people on the idea, but the company CEOs were reluctant at best. One agreed to take on creating and managing one of the utilities. Still, less than an hour later, when asked the question in a management meeting, he said it was a mistake, a statement for which he was congratulated by another CEO. Both made it clear to me later in private that the only issue was risk to their career, not the company's benefit. The utility idea died.

Jonathan can be a bulldog, and he did not let go. He asked me for alternatives in a meeting with the CEOs, and I offered the only alternative I saw: complete outsourcing of technology across the entire corporation. This was a trend then, and the leading vendor was IBM. Jonathan told me to get him an offer, and I did. Here I really went beyond the comfort zone for an advisor, and I should have realized it was a fool's errand.

IBM made a very attractive financial offer and agreed to do separate contracts with each operating company (a huge concession). The operating companies said they got the point and committed to saving even more. The deal died. I learned that even if you are the absolute boss, there are real limits to power. Would it have worked? In reality, few of these deals were ever clear-cut successes. The challenges at DMGT were major.

The savings IBM saw came from consolidation. While there would be separate contracts with each company, they were going to use a consolidated team for delivery. DMGT could always do a similar thing on its own, but then every operating executive would have a built-in excuse for non-performance. The same surely would have happened with IBM.

Eventually, I figured it out: IT was not just information technology—it was also the fudge factor to make the LTIPs. Companies sold IT projects in the budget process to gain funding, but because of the light-touch management, no one ever fully checked that the money was spent that way.

As I wrote above, IT systems need constant maintenance, but it is not immediately obvious if you skip it for a while. (A friend told me this was a recurring issue at Microsoft.) This is how tech debt increases at nearly every company. Also, there is the ability to capitalize certain expenses under certain conditions, which again boosts the LTIP payouts. Anything that touched IT went right to the ability of the managers to ensure their LTIP payments. It was the third rail of DMGT as it is at many other companies.

We heard a constant complaint about the quality of the IT people. With my colleague Peter Duffy, head of human resources, we supported an annual IT conference. It was a very good investment, but the operating people were skeptical. What became clear quickly was that, on the contrary, the IT people were really good. The operating executives were spurred to hire technology Boston Consulting Group heads who brought senior leadership to their teams, which made things even better.

The problem was product, and editorial organizations tend to have a naïve view of product. There is always tension between what the business wants and what the technology team can deliver. Moreover, you learn as you go, so revisions are inevitable. Good product takes good teamwork. In the businesses of DMGT and many other companies, the content owners were the "gods," believing they should get whatever they wanted when they wanted it. Failure was always an IT issue. DMGT is not alone in this attitude. Peter and I embarked on building up product skills and understanding. The employees loved it, and I think it helped. But the content owners never embraced the idea. In retrospect, I should have spent far more time with the content owners—if they would have seen me. I did succeed in planting the concept of a chief product officer, which I believe is critical to success today.

My role at DMGT shrank after the IBM fiasco. Anyone in a staff role is always in a position where doing what is right may cost you your job. Martin Morgan took me aside and said I was now in a role in which the operating companies needed to ask for my help before I could do anything. It also reduced my compensation. I was still a standing attendee at the Investment and Finance Committee and remained involved in multiple areas, but I was clearly more marginal than I had been.

I reviewed the technology at the Digital Property Group and helped convince their DMGT management that there was little future. That led to merging it into Zoopla, which was an enormous financial win. I helped convince Paul Dacre, the powerful editor-in-chief of the *Daily Mail*, to support creating a tablet-based product.

Most importantly, I worked very hard with McKinsey on the board presentation that led to the approval of the expansion of MailOnline, although Martin Clarke, the founder, went his own way once approved (he did thank me for the support though). Afterward, I spent a lot of time communicating where other media companies were going, especially the *Washington Post*. I also spent a lot of time on the reengineering of the Hobsons until it was sold. I helped recruit multiple players. Finally, my constant evangelism of IT architecture helped people understand the importance of modular architectures to enable rapid change.

The Investment and Finance Committee was and is the central control point at DMGT. Chaired by Jonathan, it is the decision forum for almost every major decision. The light-touch philosophy also had to comply with fiduciary duty, and the I&FC was where the two met. I never worked with a better group of people. They were dedicated and deliberate, but it was nearly impossible for any such group to deal in depth with the range of issues brought to them.

That includes acquisitions, and acquisitions were a constant stream when I first joined. Interesting businesses were bought using a mixture of cash and an earnout. A careful process was followed, and deficiencies were usually identified. A remediation plan was included in the acquisition proposal. Everything looked good.

My time spent on the I&FC was very informative about the challenges of managing a portfolio of businesses. One operating company brought forward a large software development project for approval. The business case was sound. The numbers were great. It promised future growth in revenue and profit far beyond what was required to financially justify the investment.

I caused a stir because I saw a huge red flag: the company intended to implement the project using Microsoft .Net technology. This was a subtle but critical observation. Microsoft .Net technology is like a lot of Microsoft technology: it enables mediocre to good talent to deliver good to very good results. But it is not a technology on which you should build any system-level product. Industry lore says that if building software for you to use is one, building it for others to use is three and building a platform on which others can build is ten. If you have never done this, it is very hard to accept.

While the company had a lot of good application-level technology built on .Net, the new product was entirely new. Like a contractor who built strip malls deciding to build skyscrapers. There also is a canard that there is no such thing as a great .Net developer, because no great developer would write in .Net. Alas, time would prove me right, but again—no manager not steeped in software would understand the issue. Eventually, the company succeeded. It took more money and more time than initially projected. And a change in people.

As I said above, DMGT swore by two beliefs: light-touch management because it attracted better talent; and LTIPs/earnouts because financial motivation worked. It was hard to argue with either. Two very good principles stand alone, but together they can be toxic. I see the appeal of both for a portfolio management company. Trying to manage someone else's business is almost always folly. Private equity seems to make it work, but they are more ruthless on performance, aggressive as owners, and centered on equity. None of these were going to work at DMGT.

Jonathan recognized all this, and he then did what few management teams ever do. Maybe this is a key difference between owners and managers. He changed course. Paul Zwillenberg succeeded Martin Morgan as CEO, and he quickly moved to simplify the business. He viewed the portfolio more as a private equity firm would. He looked at the companies, bet on RMS over Euromoney, and executed a divorce. He realized DMGT lacked the resources—human and capital—for such a broad portfolio, so he focused on strengthening the businesses and then began to sell off the weaker parts of the portfolio. One such asset was BuildFax, where I served as board chairman during the sale. Finally, he sold off two of the stronger companies with good timing on the valuations. The largest and last was RMS.

DMGT is now much more poised for success. As a private company, it has more flexibility to adapt and change. The scope of businesses is reduced, and the knowledge and skills necessary to manage them are similarly reduced. There are still the many challenges of adapting to our ever-changing world for a media company, but they have the foundations to succeed. I wish them well.

CONCLUSION

N 1965, THE LATE GORDON MOORE, A FOUNDER OF INTEL, made the observation that the density of semiconductors would double every year for the next ten years—a postulate he updated ten years later to every two years. That translates to a 30 percent per year reduction in cost for semiconductors, and 97 percent over a decade.

Never in history has a critical component of our economy declined in cost by so much for so long. This tenet became known as Moore's Law; it has been widely acknowledged as the main driver behind the computer revolution. (See, for example, *Measuring and Sustaining the New Economy** from the National Academy of Sciences, in which I wrote the volume on software.)

In fact, Moore's Law is far too simple to be the sole explanation for the computer revolution. Industries are composed of companies, which are organizations of people bound by a complex set of covenants and incentives. Change at the pace of Moore's Law places incredible strain on those organizations

---

*   Wessner, C., and Dale Jorgenson, ed., *Measuring and Sustaining the New Economy* (Washington: National Academy Press, 2002).

and people. Bill Joy, a co-founder of Sun, had a "law" of his own: the number of truly bright people at any company is proportional to the logarithm of the total number of employees (i.e., the percentage declines rapidly with size). A very small number of very bright people made this all happen.

As someone who was "present at the creation" and played a small part along the way, my most important takeaway is not how incredibly our technology has advanced or how dramatically it has changed our society. It is how important individuals and relationships were to the process.

Again and again, I saw that people do business with people. I saw brilliant people make an incredible difference. Yes, Moore's Law was critical, but laws take human beings to have an effect. For example, almost all of the computing devices in the world today run software derived from earlier software that was designed by one of two people: David Cutler (DEC VAX and Windows NT) or Bill Joy (Berkeley Unix).

The plain paper copier revolutionized the office. You have to be my age or older to appreciate that, but it did. The internet did it again, by maybe an order of magnitude more. Then smartphones revolutionized society. Artificial intelligence may be about to do it again.

I have been very privileged to be part of this journey. Sometimes as a bystander. Sometimes as a bit player. Sometimes as a principal. I hope I have communicated how important individual people and specific events were to making this all happen.

A recent Harvard study of lifetime satisfaction concluded that relationships—in the end—were the most important factor. I hope the examples I have included make that point around business and career success. Nothing matters more, in my opinion. I have attached an essay I wrote for a younger friend fifteen years ago as Appendix 4. The lessons in that article are still valid.

Successful leaders in my experience understand that there are only 168 hours in a week, and prioritizing your time is the most important decision you make. I have watched many leaders over many years, and to me it is clear that the most successful understood this.

There are four tasks in an organization that only the leader can perform:

- **Awareness:** The leader has to be aware of the environment in which he or she operates. In all aspects and all dimensions. The reasons for this are simple. You want your team to focus, so it is up to you to look for threats and opportunities. This is not something you can do sitting in an office. You need to talk to customers, employees, government, researchers, etc. You need to understand where you need to be. You cannot lead if you do not know where you are going.

- **Attraction:** You have to bring your organization what it needs for success. In the beginning this may be capital, but at all stages it is talent. Talent is hard. You may have to change business practices to create an environment that attracts and retains talent, especially if you need multiple talent pools. Recruiting and retaining this talent is a key responsibility. It will take a lot of your time. If you delegate it away, you likely will fail.

- **Architect**: You decide the organization structure. You decide who decides. You decide how fast decisions get made. You decide how much tolerance you have for errors versus speed of decision-making. Organizations take time to adapt, so constant change is disruptive. On the other hand, if the environment is changing rapidly, so also probably should your architecture.

- **Alignment**: This is the hard part. Every leader faces the challenge of delivering a consistent message to management or investors, employees, and customers. It would be great if all three could be different, but that is not the real world. At minimum, they must be consistent. Then, you need your team all aligned on that message. If you do not test for understanding, you will fail. Achieving alignment is the hardest task any leader faces.

Humans are quite predictable. Given a problem, they immediately convert it into another problem they know how to solve. Otherwise, they can do nothing. Unfortunately, especially as a problem is passed on, minor differences are introduced, and eventually the problem being solved may have nothing to do with the original. This is life. The leader has the job of making sure this does not happen.

I have seen many leaders fail because they convert their role into doing what they do best and do not focus on the four tasks above. We feel better about ourselves doing something well than doing something less well, even if what we are doing is not the correct priority. This is why leadership is hard.

THE AGONY OF SPRING

T*HIS CHAPTER WAS WRITTEN IN 1978 AND SUBMITTED TO HAR-
VARD MAGAZINE, WHICH AGREED TO PUBLISH IT. I received
a phone call from the late Henry Rosovsky who had been
very good to me at Harvard and who was then the Dean of the
Faculty of Arts and Sciences, a huge job. He congratulated me
on it and said it was very good and accurate. He then asked me
as a personal favor not to publish it. Obviously, editorial independence had been overstated, but I withdrew it. Rather than
write recollections of that time, I think it best now to go with the
contemporary recollections, just lightly edited. I learned a lot in
admissions, not the least of which was how to work as a team and
how to evaluate people. Please remember that this was written
over forty years ago, and many things change in that time.*

"You call it."
"Heads."
"Tails."
"Too bad."
In such fashion was decided the fate of one applicant to

Harvard College. In truth, the toss really did not matter—all that was at stake was a place on the waiting list, at Harvard as at many other colleges a prize that is at best a costless gesture. Indeed, the student may have gained by losing that bet in absentia. Otherwise, he would have thought he had a chance of being admitted, which he did not have in truth. However, he, his school and his local alumni all would have believed that he had a chance. Therein lies the truth of selective college admissions: It is a game with very high stakes, but it is a game—a game which can be played.

This is a personal memoir. It reflects nearly five years spent admitting students to Harvard and Radcliffe Colleges thirty years ago. Before and during that time I came into contact with most of what makes Harvard, well, Harvard. I also worked with admissions and financial aid officers from a number of other Eastern Private Colleges. My undergraduate education was much different—as different as a public, land-grant university can be from Harvard. I learned a lot at Harvard, formally and informally. There is no question in my mind that an undergraduate education there offers the best such experience in the United States. Note that I said experience, for the formal education elsewhere may be as good or better. But only the most self-centered academic should place much emphasis today on the value of formal training. What matters in life is what Harvard provides. While you can surely get it elsewhere, Harvard will give you it much earlier—and in concentrated doses.

I am a student of the statement "Process affects outcomes." The Harvard admissions process is a process that has been revered for years: "Let the high priests continue to do whatever they do as it works" has been the received doctrine at Harvard for nearly a quarter century. The Harvard admissions process has also generated much public interest, for rightly or wrongly Harvard is the goal for many of America's gifted high school graduates. The Supreme Court singled it out as a right way to implement Affirmative Action.

This chapter presents an analysis of the Harvard and Radcliffe Colleges admissions process, its goals and procedures. Admission to Harvard or Radcliffe is a prize worth seeking, but it should be sought somewhat in the manner of roulette in the private rooms of the casino at Monte Carlo. You have to be qualified to get in the door, so everyone does not try. But whether you win depends as much or more on luck as skill.

THE PRIZE

Each year more than 20,000 students think enough about applying to Harvard that they have their College Board S.A.T. scores sent to the Admissions Office. By the end of the admissions "season" over 12,000 students will actually apply. Why the others do not is an interesting but unanswered question. Presumably, they eliminate themselves on the basis of their scores or finances, neither of which is a certain basis for decision. This last question—who can afford a Harvard education?—continues to trouble the College today.*

These 12,000-plus applicants range widely in quality. Some are hopeless repeats. Some are stellar. Some are too good to be true—literally, although phony applications are a

---

* Not true today.

rarity and are usually easily detected. Some—but not as many as might be thought—are, in the admissions jargon, not competitive. This is not a personal reflection on the candidate; the admissions folder simply does not contain the information necessary to justify a space in the class.

Nearly half the applications are alright: strong enough to defend an admission, strong enough to probably succeed at Harvard but not so strong that the outside world would not accept a rejection. And, there are a handful of political cases of children of the rich and powerful, in Harvard and global terms, in that order of priority.

One point just made deserves reemphasis: The committee admits people primarily on the basis of paper credentials. Some great candidates are surely missed because their strengths fail to come through on those pieces of paper. Others sound much better on paper than they are. Great effort is made to secure a personal appraisal, but even so it is the paper which counts most in the end. For this reason personal contact is always valuable to an applicant for it affords the staff representative a personal perspective and new information can be obtained where the representative sees it helpful.

As I said above, Harvard does not provide a necessarily great formal education. It can be great, but for most students that likely reflects either lucky accident or strong perseverance. Great teaching is not the hallmark of the Harvard faculty, although Harvard has some truly great teachers. And some of the junior faculty and graduate students who share the teaching burden can be inspiring. After all, it is a myth that higher academic rank implies better teaching. I could never understand the claims of one Harvard competitor that its assistant professors could be great teachers after supposedly having been terrible graduate assistants the year before at Harvard.

A perhaps even greater myth is that teaching at the college level anywhere really matters. There is considerable evidence that it does not, but for academics to admit that fact would deprive them of their rationalization justifying their privileged status. One extraordinarily distinguished Harvard professor once remarked to me that the attitudes of our colleagues should not surprise me. "After all," he said, "most of them are incapable of doing anything at all valuable in the real world, so they have to make a virtue out of what they do. They call it 'scholarship.'"

An undergraduate I knew researching an article on the promotion process at Harvard asked a senior professor why his department did not actively seek great teachers. The student found his answer difficult to accept: "Because that would imply that my colleagues should also try to teach well, and they can't." Research remains the criterion for promotion. This is certainly not a condition peculiar to Harvard, but it is true. The opposite rhetoric is largely that, rhetoric. It may be true that teaching is more elusive than research so that "publish or perish" is the best rule.

While Harvard teaching may not be great, many Harvard courses are. Courses acquire lives of their own with reputations to uphold. Their massive reading lists are usually well developed. The emphasis on summary written work, say only one three-hour examination for the course, is often seen by the students as unfair or worse. Yet, both the long reading lists and the emphasis on written analysis teach by-doing skills that are extremely valuable in college, in professional school and in the real world. Studies have repeatedly shown that most colleges develop intellectual maturity in their students; these same studies show that Harvard develops it very quickly. The transformation of a student over this or her freshman year is a pleasure to watch—if all goes well. Many students will dwell at length on their intellectual experiences at Harvard, although in many cases this joy of learning is not matched in grades.

As I will return to below, the central fallacy in most discussions of Harvard education or of education generally is that what matters is what is taught, when what really matters is what is learned.

THE PROCESS

The digression above is important, for it sets the context for admissions decisions. The first rule of admissions is that very bright students are almost always admitted. Very bright means just that, another Nobel Prize winner perhaps. Ideally, such a student should have several respected professional articles to his or her credit (and some do). Without that, high 700s or an 800 on all College Board tests, perfect grades at a known secondary school plus sterling recommendations from all asserting ". . . the very best in 20 years" might be enough. Might. Standards are high, but remember that they apply only to those very few students each year admitted solely on academic grounds.

These one hundred or so students are probably about all that can or should expect really personal attention from the faculty. The interests of these students are largely academic, and Harvard offers them what they seek. The faculty is happy because they have bright students with interests in their field, however obscure or arcane. Let me emphasize that Harvard admits virtually everyone who is this bright. And it gets a very large share of the total pool of those persons.

Harvard has a freshman class of about 1600. Roughly, three in four of those admitted choose to enroll, so that the college admits about 2100 students, of which only one hundred or so are selected on purely academic grounds. No one is rejected with exceptional academic ability except in truly unusual cases, which, however, are there every year, it seems, but this leaves 2000 spaces to be filled.

The ultimate discretion open to the committee on admissions is quite limited, because the committee understands a basic truth: Harvard is the best largely because everyone believes it is the best. It is surely not the best because of its excellent teaching or any other structural reason, as many other fine colleges and universities continually stress. Thus, as little as possible must disturb the impression that Harvard is the best. Effectively, the next 1,400 to 1,600 admissions in the class must and do go to candidates perceived as "deserving" of Harvard by their respective community and the admissions committee.

To make their decisions, the committee staff first develops a profile for each applicant: he or she is assigned a rating of 1–4 (with some exceptions) on academic, extracurricular, athletic and personal strengths. By one criterion of health, the entire admissions staff is due for imminent heart attacks, for those numbers become part of their lives. Asked to describe someone's spouse, an admissions staffer is likely to reply "a 3+342." and everyone on the staff understands.

The very bright people described earlier are 1-academics. Generally, a 1-rating in any category is a virtual certainty of admission, except in athletics, to which I will return later. There is one caveat: The candidate must be able to do the (academic) work. Or, as one longtime senior staff member used to say, "... be able to do the morning exercises as well as those in the afternoon."

The brighter a candidate, the more likely the candidate will be admitted. The rule is simple and straightforward. Despite some grumblings from the Harvard faculty, this really is the policy of the committee, and objective statistics prove it. Of course, other factors help and hurt.

The easiest way to not be admitted is to be a 4-personal. Today that is described as bland personality, but it covers a multitude of sins. A handful, at best, make it in with that rating. And a frequent comment in those cases is, "I knew his mother or father, and she or he was a 4-personal too." Actually, the committee favorite in my time was 6-personal, which was formerly used to signify obnoxious or aggressive. But the privacy laws have suppressed that flavor.

The easiest way to be admitted if the candidate is not a 1-academic is to have a 2222 profile or better (i.e., one or more ratings are one). Virtually everyone so rated is admitted. These are the people who are the dream students at any college: excellent strengths across the board; bright, very bright; potential Rhodes scholars. Harvard recruits these people actively.

At the margin are those candidates rated 2333, bright but dull. About half, the more exciting half, are admitted.

But many are turned down. This is probably the better for them. If the assessment of the committee is correct, they would find themselves with no area of excellence at Harvard. They are persons whose main interest in high school has been academic excellence but who lack the academic power to excel academically at Harvard.

The committee has strong roots to the view that every student needs his or her hook into college life, some area in which to excel at Harvard. Interestingly, until Harvard and Radcliffe merged their admissions office, the Radcliffe phrase was niche. That difference told much about the difference in selection criteria. It also says why the females admitted to Harvard under a merged process were so much different.

But, in the end, the admissions criterion effectively becomes whether everyone expects a student to be admitted and whether Harvard really cares what his or her community thinks. If every year the number one student at a high school is denied admission, that community will lose faith in Harvard as the best. In most cases high schools outside of New England and New York have exalted views of what Harvard is, so that every number one does not apply. If they did, the committee would face many more tough choices than it does now.

As it is, the committee and its staff function because some accepted and acceptable decision rules define the group Harvard must accept at a size Harvard can accept. While some individual cases are argued at the margin, ninety percent or so of those rated as clear admits by the final staff reader on the folder are eventually admitted. To be nearly assured of admission a candidate has to fall into one of the favored categories on the basis of the information in the folder.

After admitting this must group, the committee has open four to five hundred spaces in the class plus the waiting list. These are political cases purely and simply. There are several thousand persons in the applicant pool who could be chosen more or less at random. The class would change very little if this rule were followed. The final selection really is random in terms of quality selection but is used to serve Harvard purpose.

Members of the admission staff fall into four categories: (1) those who understand the game but who are charged with maintaining the charade; (2) those who understand the game but have no power—they do the only rational thing and don't worry about their candidates; (3) those who really think they do something important and who try hard to do the right thing in an absolute sense; and (4) those who just don't understand. A candidate's chances for admission can vary tremendously with the group to which his or her staff representative belongs.

Indeed, a very real problem for any staff member who does understand the process is the definition of merit. Like many things, merit is in the eye of the beholder. Under different admission staff members a school or area might find its number of admitted applicants changing by a factor of two or more. Is perception by one staff member merit? It is a necessary fiction that it is.

The real problem, of course, is that while 2333s may be compared with some sense of meaning. The real choice open to the committee is between 2333s and 3222s. This choice is somewhat masked by the fact that the 2333 are heavily from Northeast suburban high schools, while the 3222s are from the Midwest, West and South. Nevertheless, the committee could easily admit many more 2333s if it chose to do so.

The reasons for not doing so are quite simple and valid. The committee is not anti-Semitic, but this charge surfaces every year in the guise of claims that the committee discriminates against Long Island and Westchester. It is true that the committee does have some implicit constraint on the number of 2333s it wants in the class. Harvard profits as do her students from heterogeneity. The goal is not to have the highest average SAT scores possible or to maximize the grade point average of Harvard classes.

Thus, the committee openly seeks diversity of all types. It is this desire which restricts the number of 2333s. Interestingly, 3222s often do much better academically than 2333s, as except for scores at the very top, SAT scores seem to predict little about grades once the verbal score reaches 550* or so. Nevertheless, the need to compare inherently different people must always be an imperfect process.

The elusive admission standards generate much concern in some students. It is not uncommon to find students who ignore all protestations to the contrary to believe that they should not have been admitted. This is very often true of thoughtful, would-be athletes who feel they must succeed in athletics to justify their presence. A close friend rejected by Harvard but thought more qualified by the student is a frequent source of his or her doubts.

---

* Because of renorming, this is probably more than a hundred points higher today.

ITS DEFENSE MECHANISMS

Politics then decides who is admitted. There is a committee, of course. It is technically a committee of the Faculty of Arts and Sciences, and the majority of its membership are senior faculty and administrators. But admissions is very time consuming because this is very necessary for the image. After all, it is much easier to tell someone that he or she was rejected after long deliberations rather than after two brief scans of his or her application credentials, especially if the latter scenario is correct, as is often true. The process is so time-consuming that it is invulnerable to attack by outsiders. Anyone who attacks a process of which he or she has never been a part is on very shaky ground when all apparent characteristics are exemplary. "Any time-consuming process must be thorough" runs the conventional wisdom.

When one well-intentioned and sincere faculty member used to challenge staff decisions, he was inevitably treated to a "40 days and 40 nights speech" having the general theme of "What right did he have to question decisions when he did not know the context in which they were made?" Only that he was appointed to the committee to do just that. But personal conflict is not the way of academia, so the faculty win a few cases to pacify them. Often, those cases are mistakes for all concerned, but they keep the process free from challenge. Besides, a faculty member can always be reminded of a mistake to discredit his or her judgment later.

The large time commitment is effective for another reason. More than once, I smiled as students were admitted in the afternoon with a lot of faculty present, only to be rejected at midnight when only a few staffers were left. The faculty members who had pushed the cases had gone home. Endurance is a very old tactic. Seldom has it been used so effectively.

In the final result, it is the admissions staff that make the decisions. To be more precise, it is the Dean of Admissions and Financial Aid who makes the decisions. Among other things, he determines who votes and counts the votes. But this is really unnecessary, as I never once saw the Dean lose a case.

Of course, no Dean personally could make all 12,000-plus decisions however much he might wish to do so, as it is physically impossible. Over time, as a result, a three-stage process has developed. First, the folders are read, as described above. The Dean selects the readers, thereby assuring that at least one person he trusts reads each folder. Second, subcommittees chaired by senior staff members consider cases by geographic area. Third, a committee chaired by the Dean makes the final decisions by reviewing the decisions of the subcommittees.

The most repeated charge against Harvard admissions is that it displays geographic preference. This is false except to the extent different areas produce different types of applicants. Beyond a few romantic cases from the rural and western parts of the US, admissions criteria are essentially uniform. A suburban high school valedictorian and student council president is not very different if the suburb is of Los Angeles or Seattle or Detroit or Boston. Spaces are distributed to the subcommittees only after the readings have been done, and they are allotted on the strength of those readings. The reason the same number tend to be admitted from an area is simply the statistical law of averages: the applicant pool and its distribution are quite stable.

Thus, a subcommittee has a number of spaces to fill and a much larger pool from which to fill them. One level of politics operates at this level: How well the staff member knows how to play committee politics. New staffers generally lose. Senior staff members do quite well. In the end, each staff member gets some people admitted largely to please him or her. Some staff members get more, some get less. It creates a valuable illusion among many staff members that they really have impact. In a sense they do, but, as far as Harvard is concerned, the choice is Tweedle-Dee and Tweedie-Dum. It is a small price to pay to keep staff interested enough to work unreasonable hours for unreasonably low pay, though they do get to work at Harvard. The illusion of choice is reinforced by always overadmitting and then progressively cutting back to the target.

This function of the subcommittee process is really incidental to its true purpose which is to identify for the Dean all the cases about which he should care. Ideally, this could be trusted to the subcommittee chairman, but the Dean gets a full review in the last stage.

ITS DISTORTIONS

Whom does the Dean have to consider? Well, first he has to keep the alumni happy. This is done by admitting 2 out of 5 of the alumni children who apply. Compared to the 1 in 6 ratio overall this keeps them at bay. "Why?" is an interesting question. Alumni children tend to be highly qualified in many cases, so that with no alumni preference the ratio might be very close to 2 in 5 anyway. Indeed, when I was there, the Dean had to put some, but not very many, alumni children in the class in the last stage to reach the 2 in 5 ratio. I suspect that most of those admitted by the subcommittees would have been admitted even if their parents had gone to Yale.

All alumni are not created equal, however, so some alumni matter more. There may be little that the Dean can do in some cases, as some applicants are hopelessly weak academically. Admitting them would only invite disaster later. Or, context may make admission impossible. But each year the Dean must see that a few applicants with dubious credentials but distinguished relatives are admitted.

Like many words in this game, context covers many sins. What it means is that Harvard does not like to make embarrassing decisions. It may make perfect Harvard sense to admit the daughter of a wealthy alumnus who has decent if not great scores and who ranks in the middle of her class. However, if there are 35 other better qualified applicants from that high school of which only 3 are being admitted, it is fairly difficult to explain to the school on other than political grounds. Merit hardly leaps to the fore as an explanation, especially, as is often the case, if all of the 35 are in the top 50 of their class.

A process that has been around as long as this one has, has developed a stable of tricks by now to solve this dilemma. One is the waiting list; another is sending the applicant to one of a small number of private schools.

The waiting list has a semi-noble purpose. Maybe, just maybe fewer than 70 percent of those admitted will choose to come. If so, Harvard will be able to admit more students later. The waiting list says you have been selected to be considered in that event. A consolation prize. You were very close. In truth, only a few students are admitted every year.

In the first instance those students tend heavily to be political cases that could not be admitted initially because of school context or similar political reasons. A few students on whom new information is obtained generally are admitted. The rest go to keep whoever is around at the time happy and to solve political problems with alumni and schools. Nobody cares very much late on a Friday afternoon in June anyway. Except the candidates.

The waiting list is probably most valuable as the costless gesture it is. Put the alumnus daughter somewhat higher in the class. and it might be possible to pacify the school with two or three waiting list spaces. The theory is that the daughter and those on the waiting list were close in quality but the extra tip for lineage allowed Harvard to admit the daughter now. This ploy works.

A good private school is really a far safer bet, however. Many of the people whose children go to those schools are people whom Harvard wants to have continue thinking that Harvard is the very best. Moreover, Harvard is more than willing to admit their children in return for the appropriate financial support, although this is never explicit. The private schools provide a gateway to Harvard for their children without disturbing the outward image of merit.

They do this in several ways. First, to be honest, they provide an excellent education. They make it at least possible in some cases for the student to be able to do college work. Second, these schools provide good support to their students. Public schools almost universally do not. This is not necessarily meant to be critical of public-school teachers and counselors. The legal environment has become increasingly hostile. They have many recommendations to write. And they frequently know very little about the student. At these private schools, however, everyone knows that these recommendations are why the schools survive. The student may not be any better, but the school makes him or her sound better. Remember that the committee acts on written record, and these schools do have a way of accentuating the positive. It keeps those unspoiled staff members happy since they still think merit is being used.

Third, these schools offer many areas for the student to find success. Thus, college applications from these schools include many areas of extracurricular and athletic interest. You don't have to be very good to play second-team junior varsity handball, but it does look nice on the application.

But these ways are minor compared to the fourth: The schools provide a beautiful context. Harvard can admit a balanced slate of applicants from the school, not disturb its image of greatness and at the same time take some weakly-qualified alumni children who would otherwise be very obvious. This is even more true when you get to waiting list spaces. Smart schools play this game and create context problems to get more students into Harvard. This ploy works sometimes too.

ATHLETICS

There is another area where merit fades: athletics. Of course, athletic as well as academic merit counts at Harvard. For example, in any given year, Harvard used to admit 60 to 80 football players. It admitted more, of course, but the football was incidental to their admission. Why so many? Harvard imposed strict limits on recruiting, and some recruited candidates turn out to be less good than anticipated. Alumni also have to be kept interested in helping to recruit, and the way to do that is to admit young athletes they have recruited. Coaches also have little reason to downplay a self-defined football player who is easy to admit but not a great football player in their judgment.

Another reason that the number admitted had to be so large is that the coach has no scholarships to use as discipline. Financial aid did not and does not depend upon a student playing sports. A student can quit whenever he or she wants. This is a good theory, and I support the principle in abstract. However, there are costs to big-time football—Harvard football is not that different in atmosphere than elsewhere in the NCAA Division I—and Harvard drops many of these costs randomly on those players admitted who never make it in sports. I once found myself simultaneously recruiting three young men all of whom were told that each was the leading prospect for one key position, something I knew was false from an unexpected visit to the coach's office where the depth chart was on display.

Of course, it was impossible that all three were the top prospect, but the disappointment came later when they were all safely at Harvard. The result of not having scholarships is less certainty in both recruiting and retention. Coupled with this uncertainty in admission, this leads to great pressure by the coach for a large squad to minimize risk. One unfortunate byproduct of this is preference of coaches in making the resulting choices among that large pool for those who place athletics first. This is natural. It is not official policy. But the informal signals all run this way. The result is a de facto professional squad with a large protective cover to hide their excessively non-academic character. Recent changes which greatly narrow the number of athletic spots only increases the pressure, and athletes are increasingly an isolated community performing for a narrow fan base.

Selective perception operates powerfully to isolate the athletic success cases from the failures. Failure is too strong a term, perhaps, for all that happens is that someone who wanted to play did not. But sport is a terribly important part of the American life, and to minimize the effect on these young men and women is unjustified callousness. In the end the administration and the alumni want winning teams. The tragedy is that very little is done to see that those who provide those victories get their reward from Harvard. Instead, the faculty often dismiss them as jocks not worthy of their time. This prophecy is easily self-fulfilling. And those alumni who were great friends for four years can turn deaf ears when an athlete graduates and can no longer provide 50-yard-line seats.

Granting no special treatment to athletes sounds like high principle. But Harvard admits no other marginal academic group which it expects to spend 20, 40, 60, or more hours per week in season (and out of season more and more) doing a non-academic assignment. The real reason for the lack of concern about athletes, I suspect, is intellectual snobbery: Many faculty members cannot comprehend any satisfaction from earning a B in a course. Indeed, I would wager that many faculty view athletics as something done solely for money. Certainly, the money issue is never far from the surface in any discussion of college athletics.

All things considered, however, I don't think that Harvard is any worse than any other college. In fact, it is probably better than most. What is troubling is the pretension. All the Ivies play the game of football recruiting seriously. NCAA rules are inevitably broken by everyone—the only question is degree—and, in my experience, violations at Harvard were generally trivial. The temptation to cheat is great, however, when your competition does not play by all the rules. And they do not.

"To try to do something which is inherently impossible is always a corrupting enterprise."* That advice deserves to be deeply contemplated by all involved in college athletics today. Grown men and women with families and retirement to consider have to produce winning teams. To tell them to do that in a morally-uplifting way to the benefit of all amateur athletics is folly. The corruption it induces dirties us all.

A GROWING THREAT

The greatest threat to Harvard and its standing comes in the area of costs. $40,000 per year is a lot to pay for an education. Fewer and fewer parents are going to be able and willing to pay that amount. Harvard does offer financial aid to need to all who are admitted. and it has gone farther than any college in offering aid to both the students and to his or her parents.

---

* The situation with athletics is quite different today in many ways. Remember this was written in 1978.

200

But the awarding of aid rests upon a needs analysis system regulated by the Federal government. One of the main intentions of the Federal rules is to deny aid to the very people to whom Harvard wants to give aid. Is it good public policy to give Federal funds to a $150,000 income family to send a child to Harvard? I can't answer that question, but the obvious Harvard answer is yes. Congress may well think differently.

More importantly, much of the aid now being dispensed is probably going to families not telling the whole truth. The system is sufficiently inane that it encourages families to lie. Some families are lying to the IRS already; it is only continuing a pattern. Many of the students on aid are from divorced families whose ability to pay is obscure at best. In general, the payoff is enormous, the risk of exposure slight and the penalty if caught minimal. Under these circumstances, some fraud is inevitable, although legal games may be even more effective.

But it may be that system which destroys Harvard. Measured academic ability and income are highly correlated in the United States. The students with the scores that Harvard and similar colleges seek come from the very families finding it most difficult to finance that type of education. Those richer and poorer are not, but the bulk of people with the skills these colleges want come from the broad upper-middle-income group. If the selective colleges lose them, these colleges will become the haven of the rich with some poor.

MINORITY ADMISSIONS

The social and institutional pressures over the last decades to increase enrollments of minority group members at Harvard and Radcliffe have presented the committee with a unique challenge by expanding the scope of diversity they had to achieve. Despite considerable success, the committee is still viewed by many as doing too little. A *Harvard Crimson* article explored the issues at length. The general theme of the article was that Harvard could do more, that there was a vast untapped pool waiting to be tapped. In this the article voiced often repeated but little substantiated charges.

Perhaps our society does rely too much on standardized tests, and they surely contain an element of cultural bias— perhaps a large element. But those who focus their attacks on tests and admissions offices conveniently ignore an even more basic truth: The entire educational system is culturally biased, and Harvard education reflects these biases strongly.

In other words, that the tests are a biased measure of some innate level of talent does not necessarily mean that they are a biased estimate of the probability of success at Harvard. As a result, within broad ranges standardized test scores are a first measure by which admissions decisions are reached.

Very few students of any race, male or female, score in the high 700s or 800 on the SAT verbal examinations. These students always receive close scrutiny before they are ever rejected, but one in three are. At the other end, there is little evidence that scores above 550 differentiate academic success, so only if the verbal score is in the low 500s or below is it really an issue.

The problem is that there are not countless thousands of minority students with scores over 550 (largely because there are few students with high scores from other than upper-middle-income and upper-class families), nor are there large numbers of female engineers with high math scores or good football linemen with good scores. The US is a very large nation, but the pools for many types of students are very small.

As a result, Harvard recruits minority students heavily, so heavily that alumni (who think alumni preference is fine) and others often complain that too much is done. In terms of the total pool Harvard does probably better in percentage terms than it does for many other attractive candidate pools.

This process is tempered with understanding: The inner-city youth with 400 scores is admitted if the rest of the folder is positive. The bright minority girl with high scores but terrible grades is rejected just as all other such candidates are rejected.

In short, the committee does its job relatively well. More is better—even the staff would agree, but to admit more, more must apply—with the credentials to survive a university the committee does not rule. Those dissatisfied with the current outcome usually demand separatism.

Yet separatism—a separate recruiting and admission process—would fail at Harvard unless space were preallocated, something now surely illegal. The minorities and others pressing for more separate roles should take a lesson from the merger of male and female admissions. More women were admitted when the staff merged, unifying goals. Every protest gives the staff further reason to think of minorities as a goal for others—not for them, but it should be high-priority for each and every member. Cooperation not conflict will yield a far higher return.

Following the Bakke decision the media focused on the stability of the numbers of minorities admitted as evidence that there really was some hidden quota for minorities. There is surely a lower bound below which the committee would go only if the applicant pool were terribly weak, but that bound is below the current cutting edge of the class. In other words, it is not a binding constraint. If there is any quota, it comes much earlier in the recruitment process, and presumably the Court sanctified that.

At the same time, this fact is why other colleges offered umbrage at the decision. Harvard needs no quotas because it can recruit enough qualified applicants to meet almost any goal. Other institutions are not so lucky.

UNDERGRADUATE EDUCATION

Asked by me his reaction to the core curriculum that had then just been adopted by Harvard, a Yale professor of international stature replied, "A core? Yale has always had a core." I think he was right. It really was not clear, however, what goals Harvard set for its graduates—beyond giving money—in recent years. A Harvard degree meant only that you were admitted and little else.

Student unhappiness over the core was widespread—but with little foundation in fact. For many students little changed—one or two courses, perhaps. For some marginal students the change was more marked. The greatest impact fell on students whose minds were as narrow as they were brilliant.

While the core may have been beneficial, it may have been so inadvertently. The concern throughout seemed to be more on what was taught rather than on what was learned. The faculty probably believe that experiences they offer are the best part of Harvard. They clearly are for some, but for most it is those experiences outside the classroom but perhaps intensely intellectual which have the greatest impact.

I mention the core here for two reasons. First, it is necessary that Harvard change with the times (better yet, lead them) to maintain its image as the best. The core placed Harvard in lockstep with the return to structure in education. Second, in subtle ways the core altered Harvard and its admissions process. It was clearly a step, albeit a small one, back from diversity.

CONCLUSIONS

As everyone goes to college, the value of a college degree declines. Harvard economist Richard Freeman has written widely on this point. But the value of a Harvard degree increases. Another Harvard economist, Michael Spence, has written a seminal book on this general phenomenon. But can something so valuable be controlled privately? Especially when that means that admission requires wealth. For all the faults—if you want to call them that—the Harvard admissions process works. To the extent it can, it is fair and impartial. The distortions are probably a small price to pay. A governmental bureaucracy could only be worse. The nadir would be a situation such as currently exists in some countries where court suits over examination scores by question are already common. The tragedy, of course, is that with an academic-merit-only admissions policy Harvard would soon cease to be what it is.

ARCHITECT AND DISTRIBUTE

PUBLISHED FEBRUARY 18, 1992

ARCHITECT AND DISTRIBUTE IS THE CENTRAL MANAGEMENT PHILOSOPHY FOR SUN MICROSYSTEMS, INC. As a manager or executive of Sun Microsystems, you are expected to manage your people and your responsibilities according to the principles of Architect and Distribute. The goal of this paper is to outline those principles and explain their importance to you and to Sun.

Architect and Distribute will provide Sun with significant competitive advantage. These principles will yield higher quality, more job satisfaction and lower costs. Like any large organization, Sun is a very complicated and dynamic system. As we move our computer systems from uniprocessor machines to multiprocessing systems, we recognize the complexity involved. In many ways, Sun is a many-thousand-way multiprocessing system today, as each employee represents one node in a very complex and interdependent system.

When Sun was a small company, employees were encouraged to solve problems on their own. This is the spirit which helped make us successful, and we want to encourage it today. But there is a problem. Today we are a global company with countless complex interdependencies. An action which seems so obviously correct may be equally obviously incorrect in some other context, when these interdependencies are considered. The interdependencies may cross many international boundaries and time zones. Or, they may reflect the complex interactions of tactics and long-term strategy. In any case, it is difficult for any one employee today, even Scott, to know himself or herself the right answer strictly on the basis of his or her own knowledge, or that of the team working the issue.

The goal of Architect and Distribute is to empower the decision-maker closest to all the facts to make the decision by making sure that he or she, as much as possible in advance of the need, has all the information needed to make the right decision for the company locally and globally, now and for tomorrow. This imposes obligations on the decision-maker as well as on all Architects: the decision-maker is expected to make the right decision for the company as a whole balancing both short-term and long-term interests while the Architects are expected to communicate clearly through their Architectures the information the decision-maker requires. Both of these obligations are proactive: ignorance is not an excuse.

What complicates this is that every decision-maker is also an Architect. Architectures do not flow down from the top like lava: they interweave at almost every opportunity. As a result, Architects must follow an orderly process in establishing and communicating their architectures, and decision-makers must similarly follow an orderly process as they implement through the governing architectures. It is this orderly process which will guarantee that the architectures interweave rather than conflict and that decisions will be made for the best interests of the company overall, balancing both short-term and long-term interests. Decisions without process are almost surely bad.

We must make Architect and Distribute work at Sun! If we do, we will be able to sustain the culture which has helped us in our first ten years through the next ten or even longer. By letting those most affected by change and most knowledgeable about the situation manage change we will improve our ability to change. We will enhance job and career satisfaction at all levels of the company. Because we will avoid unnecessary staffs to communicate and to check and because we will be able to make decisions faster, we will lower our costs. Most importantly, we will make better decisions.

Architect and Distribute means competitive advantage for the company and improved job satisfaction for you and your employees. Please understand it. Please use it. Please live it.

PHILOSOPHY

The major objective of Architect and Distribute is to achieve coordination without bureaucracy. Bureaucracies or administrators generally have a bad name but exist nearly everywhere for a very good reason: they are as invaluable as they can be frustrating and counterproductive. In a complex, global organization, decision-makers naturally will not know all they need to make the correct long-term and short-term, local and global decision. If all decision-makers could be trusted to seek out the full context for their decisions and if all Architects could be trusted to carefully define and communicate the contexts for which they are responsible, we would not need a bureaucracy. Architect and Distribute then is fundamentally about *trust*.

What valuable functions does central administration perform? It ensures that orderly process is followed, typically by enforcement. It maintains the consistency of decisions across the company over time. It examines decisions in the context of multiple time frames from short-term to the very long-term. It protects the interests of all internal and external constituencies. None of these are necessarily bad. Most of the time they are all good. We want them. But we want them without the accompanying costs of overhead and constraints.

At Sun, we want to substitute shared values and written architectures for bureaucracy. We want to empower those closest to the decision to act. We want to encourage global planning and local implementation with strong cross-functional integration within consistent frameworks for decision-making and execution. These are the outcomes we seek when we stress Architect and Distribute. The Japanese economy since the end of World War II has perhaps been the greatest example of Architect and Distribute, where individual decision-makers consistently make those decisions best for the overall economy with little, albeit effective, centralized coordination.

Another way to consider Architect and Distribute is to

remember that, at its core, any business is a cascade of covenants between people and nothing more. In the United States, by law a public corporation, like Sun, must be managed for the best interests of its shareholders as represented by its Board of Directors. Thus, the fundamental covenant that is struck is between the management team and the Board. The choice of the word covenant, however, is deliberate, for covenant implies a two-way agreement with buy-in and support. Thus, a cascade of covenants balances both tops-down and bottoms-up processes, because agreement is implied at every level.

In a large, global company like Sun these covenants are complex and dynamic. At each level, new details, new constraints, new opportunities all become apparent. A seemingly simple covenant to increase earnings per share by, say, 15% next year manifests itself in literally thousands of subsidiary decisions. Architectures establish the processes to create and maintain those covenants, and, as do covenants, architectures cascade.

Every manager is an architect and needs an architecture. It is not possible in an Architect and Distribute environment for a manager to be successful otherwise, as the necessary information will not have been communicated or received. All of these architectures must be consistent as well as balance global, corporate requirements against operating company and geographic requirements.

All of the preceding suggests the following definition: An architecture is the minimum set of written direction that is both necessary and sufficient to enable the next layer of decisions to be made and implemented in a consistent fashion.

Every Sun manager needs to understand this definition and the rights and responsibilities it imposes. We want architects to follow a principle of parsimony: Create an architecture only where one is required. We want everyone to follow the governing architectures.

MANAGEMENT PRACTICE

Architects must communicate and enforce their architectures and understand and comply with any higher-order architectures. This is a two-way obligation. If you have architectural responsibility, you must seek out higher-order architectures within which you must operate, request them if they do not exist, clarify them as necessary and then build upon them. Similarly, if you develop an architecture, you must seek out those who it affects and get their input, communicate it clearly to them and quickly resolve conflicts.

In short, Architects must develop their architecture in a participatory process. This is a good point at which to discuss the role of consensus at Sun: Consensus has no place at Sun! A participatory process does not mean consensus: there is one clear, responsible decision-maker who is expected to make the correct decision for the company as a whole balancing both long-term and short-term interests. He or she is required to obtain input from all affected parties and, as necessary, to hear open debate on the subject. Great decisions are seldom, if ever, the result of consensus. They are often the outcome of spirited debate.

Architects must document their decisions in writing with appropriate policies and processes to communicate and implement them. Decisions not documented in writing are not decisions, for they are inherently open to so much interpretation as to be meaningless. Documentation which is not clear not only can erode the strength of the decision but can also make it far worse than it would be without a decision. It may frequently take longer to document a decision than to make it.

Architects must communicate their decisions clearly to all affected parties. The obligation is on the Architects to ensure understanding. Sending a decision by electronic mail is an important first step in communication, but it is seldom enough. Architects test for understanding, clarify as required and republish as necessary. Similarly, a decision-maker required to act on an architecture he or she finds unclear has the obligation to seek out the Architect and obtain clarification.

Decisions, policies and process are expected to be followed throughout the company. They are not suggestions. People are expected to be able to expect that they will be followed once published. Thus, when an Architect publishes something, he or she is taking on the obligation of seeing that the published decision is implemented (or changed in a defined way). At Sun, we expect the Architects to responsibly enforce their decisions. The Architect is the policeman, the prosecutor, the jury and the judge by design. With great power comes great responsibility—both ways. The less inspection, the more trust is implied, and therefore the greater the breach of trust when an architecture is violated.

All parties to any dispute are expected to escalate conflict sooner rather than later. Conflict is bad; escalation is not. The need to escalate means that the relevant Architects have not properly done their jobs or that there is an issue which truly needs to be resolved at a higher level. In either case, escalation puts the decision in the hands of the correct decision-maker. Escalation is not an admission of failure by those escalating and must not be seen that way in the organization. Not escalating wastes incredible time and energy and can greatly reduce the quality of work life.

The only constant at Sun remains change. Thus, an Architect has the obligation of constantly refining the architectures for which he or she is responsible and for constantly testing the architectures within which he or she operates. Architectures will be dynamic. However, revisions cannot be arbitrary and must be made through a reasonable, participatory process.

STYLE GUIDE

How do we want managers to behave at Sun? The first rule of behavior is straightforward and simple: No surprises! Almost every question on management behavior can be resolved by reference to this Rule 1. Those affected by your architectures should not be surprised by their contents, implementation or revisions. Those Architects with responsibility for your areas of action should not be surprised by your implementations of their architectures.

Again, the responsibilities are always both ways. When you make a decision, no materially-affected party should be surprised even though they may be very unhappy with your decision.

Rule 2 is equally simple: "Not me" is never an answer. If you identify an issue, you are responsible for seeing that it is resolved; you may be the wrong person to resolve it, but you are the right person to see that the correct decision-maker resolves it. If you own making something happen, you own all aspects of it including consequences on others. You own outcomes. These may take escalation. These may be an extra burden on you. However, if we do not follow this rule, we will build in bureaucracy. This again is a simple issue of trust.

Rule 3 has only three words: Communicate in writing. However, these are very powerful three words. First, your obligation is to communicate, which means that the receiving party must both receive and understand your message. Communication is the responsibility of the sender. Second, communicating in writing forces the clarity of thought necessary for crisp implementation while creating the shared history and templates on which we can build in the future.

Architect and Distribute will work only if we work at it every working day. It is as much a State of Mind as anything else. These three rules provide a very powerful style guide that will keep us an efficient, effective organization.

PROCESS GUIDELINES

Written, agreed architectures are required. Only by writing down an architecture do you indicate its limits. The resulting uncertainty from having an unwritten architecture will drive decisions to the center and slow them substantially. Architectures which are not agreed will not be followed and will introduce confusion and conflict. If you cannot reach agreement, escalate.

Similarly, decisions should be in writing and agreed through a participatory process. The key to making this work is the use of decision documents which institutionalize not only the decision but the reasons and the process. Decision documents should clearly and concisely state the matter to be decided with some context so others can understand the impact of the decision. For example, placing an order for an ASCII is a different question if the implication is that without the order we cannot make our revenue goals.

Decision documents should list the alternatives and evaluate the relative costs and benefits of each. Alternatives excluded from consideration should be listed with the reasons for their exclusion. The documents should state fairly the views of all interested parties. They should make a recommendation with the reasons for that recommendation and define the process for reaching closure including, most importantly, committing to a date on which the decision will be published.

Decision-makers should orient their activities towards effective decision-making and not meetings, presentations and data collection. They should publish their decision process in advance and specify the minimum set of data, tools, etc. which is both necessary and sufficient to make the decision. Making people fetch rocks is debilitating to the entire organization. If a problem seems too complicated, you are probably looking at it from the wrong level: go higher or lower.

Decision-makers should solicit all relevant input and publish a decision document. They should then decide in a timely, participatory fashion. They should document and publish the decision and promptly resolve or escalate conflicts. Making a decision is both a right and an obligation at

Sun: You are responsible for seeing that all considerations have been heard. See Rule 2 above. In particular, decision-makers are responsible for building in time for relevant Architects to participate and provide input or direction as required. It is not acceptable to create a situation of business necessity to force an Architect to make a particular decision. At minimum, the relevant Architects have the powers of the British monarch: to warn, to advise and to be consulted.

CLOSING

At their best, the principles of Architect and Distribute outlined in this paper will help keep Sun a great company for our shareholders and our employees. At their worst, they provide cover for introducing all of the costs of bureaucracy with few, if any, of the benefits. The key to achieving the former is trust. In an Architect and Distribute model of a business, there are not checkers: We are relying upon every manager and every executive to check himself or herself constantly for adherence to these principles. If you want clarification on any issue, please discuss it with your manager. We need you to understand and support this incredibly strategic direction for Sun. Thank you.

MANAGING CHANGE IN THE INFORMATION AGE AT SUN MICROSYSTEM

PUBLISHED IN 1993

SUN MICROSYSTEMS, INC., IS A 12-YEAR-OLD COMPANY WITH ABOUT 13,000 EMPLOYEES IN 13 BUSINESS UNITS AND OVER $4 BILLION IN TOTAL REVENUES FROM ITS WORLDWIDE OPERATIONS. Known for technology innovation, Sun has traditionally spent more than 10 percent of revenue on research and development. A continuing challenge is determining the right amount of funding for R&D, but the company's overall challenge is managing by and for change.

The company competes in the rapidly changing workstation industry, in which the average product life is 12 to 18 months. Nearly 95 percent of Sun's revenue comes from products that did not exist two years ago. This rapid pace drives many other changes. For example, Sun's total factory-output capacity three years ago was about $4.5 billion.

Today that figure is $14 billion, mainly as a result of changes in production processes.

Sun changes its business processes every three years, which means employees have to change their skills about 20 percent every year. Sun lives, breathes, and manages change every day. This scope and pace of changes has meant reengineering virtually every business process and system, including employee training and management practices.

Bill Joy, vice president of technology and a Sun co-founder, has stressed from the company's beginning that change is the only constant. A management philosophy based on constant change is fundamental for a startup company, but managing constant change becomes more difficult when a company reaches Sun's size. As long as Sun continues to drive change, its competitors are responding. If the competitors are driving change, Sun is responding, making the company inward-focused, which leads to centralized management and bureaucracy—management by process rather than management by results.

Management by results means driving the decision-making process to people closest to the decisions that must be made. A large corporate management staff can neither know enough to direct decision-making at multiple levels, nor respond quickly enough to make the right decision. Four key components of managing by and for change are electronic mail (e-mail), trust, architectures, and incentive compensation.

E-MAIL

Sun's 13,000 employees are linked over a global network that comprises more than 20,000 Sun workstations and other computers. Everyone in the organization is interconnected, and the primary link among all these people is e-mail. Sun employees generate 1 million e-mail messages a day, meaning that each employee receives an average of 80 messages a day. In truth, the total received varies widely but executives receive 50–100 messages routinely. Some of the messages are for employee-to-employee communication, some are critical, some informational. Some require response; some are best ignored.

The bottom-line, however, is that Sun actually uses e-mail to run the company. Reading, drafting and answering e-mail is a key part of the job for almost every employee. This use of e-mail allows the company to reduce the time it takes to make decisions. The temptation is to answer your e-mail right away, which facilitates change and its management. This immediacy fosters honesty. For example, if you envision a problem in a suggested procedure, you'll respond quickly and mention it early, before the problem becomes magnified later in the process.

Members of the management team try to answer their e-mail throughout the day. All sides of an issue can be "heard" within the space of a few hours, regardless of the participants' locations. E-mail has enabled Sun to participatively make important strategic decisions in days rather than months.

Another advantage of e-mail is rumor control. Rumors very often spread faster than fact, and e-mail can allow a rumor worldwide circulation within hours. However, e-mail also brings rumors out into the open quickly so that people can address them quickly.

On the other hand, e-mail can also kill a good idea almost instantaneously. When first put forward, most ideas are flawed. An unrefined idea, proposed on e-mail, is easy to attack. It is possible for a group to band together, instantly assail the idea's few, possibly minor flaws, and eliminate the idea before it has a chance to flourish. Upward delegation is also very easy over e-mail, even though upward delegation flies in the face of our architect-and-distribute philosophy (see below).

Sun's e-mail culture is so important that the company could not function without it. A primary challenge is for employees to realize the importance of e-mail and use it accordingly. It is one of the challenges of and most important tools for managing change at Sun. The instantaneous communication that allows Sun to change quickly comes at a price. The company spends over $110 million per year on the information infrastructure that is crucial for communicating, educating, and driving the company forward. While there may be some inefficiencies, by opting for ubiquitous network access, we believe we have been able to lower the network costs significantly per user.

Sun employees tend to duplicate data rather than share it, as would be the case in a centralized management model. The company has sacrificed some of the efficiencies of central management for a modular approach that allows faster response to change. At Sun, there is a belief that "you can never have too much modularity."

LOOSELY COUPLED, HIGHLY ALIGNED

Sun is now attempting to apply the best aspects of instantaneous communication to employee training and empowerment. Traditional training methods, such as classes and management training, are inefficient because they are broad-based and lack immediacy. Sun's goal is to train people by fostering self-education. Self-education requires fast access to information at the time and place of need.

For example, all of Sun's employee handbooks, product literature, and other information employees need day to day in online in a graphical format. Employees can get procedural instructions or modify their benefits packages and 401K plan online.

Employees were spending 10 to 20 minutes a day trying to track down this kind of information. These new approaches save time, making more employees more productive. It enhances their sense of self-sufficiency, and self-sufficiency is self-esteem. Self-esteem translates into productivity.

This training approach comes from pressure to support the day-to-day interpersonal ad hoc communication that drives business. Sun believes in maximizing the amount of self-management in the system. If people know what the rules are and feel that they can manage their piece of the business—knowing that all pieces have to be self-integrating—they will have a greater sense of self-esteem. If they don't know the rules, they will feel disempowered. Their frustration will show up in poor business results.

With so many separate businesses, Sun has concluded that it cannot run from the center. The company has to depend on lots of teams—autonomous entities that cooperate together. Sun calls this structure "loosely coupled but highly aligned."

Loosely coupled means that employees have the freedom to act and feel confident in their actions. At the same time, they can be responsive to other employees and the company's needs. If they know they're going in the same direction, with the same values, they will stay highly aligned, focusing on the same overall goals. The challenge for Sun and every business is to maintain a loosely coupled, highly aligned structure.

ARCHITECT AND DISTRIBUTE

For about a year, Sun has been stressing an overriding management philosophy, practice, and style guide called "architect and distribute." Sun believes that the architect-and-distribute philosophy represents the way to manage change in the information age and achieve success in the 1990s. This philosophy will help the company build self-esteem and trust among employees and, above all, make Sun an effective global competitor.

Architect-and-distribute is based on these principles:

1. Achieve coordination without bureaucracy.
2. Substitute shared values and written "architectures" for bureaucracy.
3. Ensure that people understand up front what the rules and guidelines are.
4. Empower those closest to decisions to act.
5. Encourage global planning and local implementation.
6. Encourage people from across the company to work in teams.

7. Provide a consistent framework for decision making.
8. Provide a framework for consistent education.

Fundamentally, any business is a set of covenants among people about their objectives and the resources to accomplish those objectives. Sun is using what it calls architectures to create policies and process by which all employees can establish and maintain these covenants and trust one another. This system creates tension, but it also offers a mechanism for resolving it. The company wants to drive conflict into the open so that people can disagree. One purpose of these architectures is to force people to escalate issues—to get senior management to address problems early and understand them, because senior managers are the ones who need to resolve the problems. The goal is to arrive at architectures by participation, not by consensus.

What Sun means by an architecture is the minimum set of written directions that is both necessary and sufficient to enable the next layer of decisions to be made and implemented in a consistent fashion.

Minimum: the architects should not intrude in a decision process unless the company has a vital stake in that particular decision.

Written: architectures that aren't written down aren't architectures, because they're fluid. Necessary: the architecture has to be important enough to implement.

Sufficient: it has to contain enough information for the next-level decision-maker, so that decisions won't be delegated upward. It does no good to make decisions that cannot be implemented, and it does no good to implement decisions inconsistently.

Architects have to understand and comply with higher-order architectures, but architectures can be bottom-up as well as top-down. People have to develop architectures through a participatory process, not through consensus. Lack of dissent means that the participants haven't addressed all the issues and tradeoffs.

Every manager should have architectures to impart to people below, and these architectures should be consistent with those from above. But these are not orders. They are agreements among people, based on mutual discussion and participation.

Because Sun is a very change-oriented company, however, not all employees understand the concept of architectures and of documenting them. People will say, "Why is it worth writing down? It's going to change anyway." If it isn't documented in writing, people aren't accountable. For architect-and-distribute to work, people need to communicate with each other.

Sun does business by e-mail, but the architect-and-distribute philosophy states that communication does not mean simply sending an e-mail ends your responsibility. Communicate mean that you test for understanding and make sure that the person on the receiving end really comprehends the message you just sent. This is part of the participatory process by which architectures are created and implemented.

To live and work according to this philosophy requires what Sun calls a style guide. The first rule in this guide is, *no surprises*. Surprises during the decision-making process lead to bad faith, and then to problems. As a Sun employee, you can't make a decision if management hasn't provided the direction, the architecture, you need in order to decide. It then becomes your decision to push the decision up. Everyone has to alert others to problems. Self-inspection has to be the rule.

Good decision-making means focusing on the decision, not on preparation for meetings or presentations in them. Specify what the process is in advance, specify the data you need in order to make the decision, solicit all relevant input, carefully consider the alternatives, make the decision, document and publish the decision, promptly resolve or escalate conflicts. It is crucial to write down your decisions, because management tends to filter out the reality of conflict and dissent in order to arrive at a political solution.

To guard against politicization of decision making, Sun is trying to operate with a corporate staff of 100. Through reassignments, the company has reduced the total corporate staff from nearly 1,500 to about 100. I run an 1,100-person systems organization, and I've reduced the central staff to 20. Architects who have large staffs will try to manage through people and directives, not through ideas and results.

Overall, the company is trying to scale down its levels of management. One way to accomplish that is to follow the rule of 11 which states that every Sun manager must have at least 11 direct reports. Sun believes that the appropriate number in the information age is 11 or more, rather than 7 or 6 or 5. The difference between a rule of 11 and a rule of 7 is a couple of layers of management.

The rules of 11 and 100 make it fairly easy to keep the

company loosely coupled. The question is how to stay highly aligned. The answer is, architect and distribute. Sun is trying to do that through this management process and this management structure.

INCENTIVE COMPENSATION

In order to motivate its managers, Sun had developed an incentive-compensation plan for which about 3,000 of the 13,000 employees are eligible. Instead of having to attain five generic, "motherhood" goals, however, Sun managers have 25 specific auditable goals. The problem with a small number of general goals is that results are difficult or impossible to measure, or they take too long to reach.

The initial reaction of some Sun managers was, "If we're going to have that many goals, then they have to be easy to achieve." The covenants on which people eventually settled was that managers receive 100 percent of their compensation if they achieve 20 of the goals.

This practice is quite different from traditional compensation theory. Sun is admitting that failure is part of the plan. Not every manager will meet all of the goals. In 1992, the average number of goals achieved was 19. For vice presidents, for example, the incentive compensation is targeted at 40 percent of base salary, which can double if performance is outstanding.

Sun also has a common corporate financial objective, which must be attained for anyone to make incentive compensation. Incentive compensation is a powerful motivator for maintaining alignment in the loosely coupled organization.

CONCLUSION

Over the last four years, Sun has realized that the company can manage change or change can manage the company. To be in charge, you have to plan and invest for change. You have to build change into the plans and the structure. In the information age, managing for change is difficult, but the alternatives are worse.

APPENDIX 4

SUCCEEDING IN ADULTHOOD: ADVICE I WISH I HAD

PUBLISHED IN *MEDIUM* IN 2013

I HAVE REACHED THAT MAGIC AGE WHEN PRONOUNCEMENTS ARE TAKEN AS WISDOM REGARDLESS OF THEIR MERITS OR UNDERLYING THOUGHT. A scary proposition but one which has so far not weighed me down that much. In this I learned from the master, John Kenneth Galbraith. As you pass through life, you learn many things. The most important things are often totally disconnected from what is taught, something which academics may understand but are loath to study.

If you are a twenty-something concerned about having a successful career, what are the key skills you need? I will not cover functional skills except to say that any person today requires knowledge of systems and how to create, maintain, and operate them. Although it may not seem apparent at this stage, life itself is a system with an intricate web of interconnected parts. You will learn why commitments are so important: It is because broken commitments are so costly, as is dealing with maybe.

Success in any field, with rare exception, requires dealing with people under uncertainty and with limited time and resources, and some canonical principles govern. The most basic tenet of leadership is that you first have to know where you are going. You would be surprised how often leaders do not or are misguided. With the right destination, leadership is actually relatively easy. Without it, success is impossible.

The best career advice I ever read was simple: six months, five years, tombstone. Step one: figure out what really matters to you, what you want as goals for your life. Step two: figure out how to make the most of what you have and where you are. Step three: make a set of concrete objectives five years out that get you from here to there. Repeat every THREE years—because things change. Shit happens. If you get an MBA, you more or less get told this in every class.

The hardest part of any plan is almost always the here-to-there piece, but neither of the other two steps is simple. We all lie to ourselves, and when we think about what we want, we are even more likely to do so. You have to figure out what you want by analyzing your own behavior, by looking back on what you do, not on what you would like to think you would be doing. Two paths work in my experience: A weekend away with one or two very close friends to talk about life in absolute confidence or a letter to yourself. Hint: if you will let anyone else read the letter, you have not been honest enough and should start over.

The process will help you acquire a fundamental skill:

learn how to solve backwards and not forwards. Figure out your objectives, survey your resources and constraints and then develop a plan to achieve them. Simply doing a little bit better from where you are just does not get you there, though it is perhaps the most common business strategy in the world. As you develop your plan, don't start with the most optimistic set of assumptions: start with the worst case. If you can build a plan then, you have the confidence to move forward.

I have seen multiple studies on organizational success and failure. Surprisingly, well-conceived, incremental goals are often not met, while BHAGs (big, hairy, aggressive goals) that seem almost impossible are achieved. Why? BHAGs are self-organizing. The troops need much less direction and coordination. Everyone knows where to go. Selecting where you are taking your people is an art as much as a science.

Plans are invaluable because they make you do planning. They almost always are wrong, but the knowledge and confidence they build is what lets leaders deal with the real world as it plays out. The real world is only a special case (as I was taught in graduate school), but it is a very important one. For most of my career, I was taught and taught that success required keeping three words in order: ready, aim, fire. That is still true but not for all businesses. When you have the ability to quickly iterate your products or services, it is increasingly apparent that oftentimes "Ready, Fire, Aim" is the dominant order because customer feedback is so much more important than anything else. And some now claim "Fire, Aim, Ready" is best.

Inevitably, you will need to do more than you have

resources available. A key to doing this is to learn to manage via an AGENDA as opposed to a SCHEDULE. By agenda, I mean you need to know what you need to accomplish and by when. Schedule means you work through this list in a systematic way with planned tasks. You do three times as much if you simply take advantage of events as they occur to accomplish your tasks. A three-minute chance meeting can replace a scheduled hour meeting with tons of overhead to coordinate. Sometimes you need to fall back to the schedule for some things, but learning how to achieve things by managing your agenda is a fundamental key to success.

You need metrics: you have to define what is success and what is failure. If you don't, you are probably not doing anything. To get great performance you also need inspection and have to learn to welcome it. I learned a fundamental lesson at Xerox: quality matters. The costs of not doing something perfectly are huge in any system. The Japanese learned this decades ago and trounced business after business. The Asian economies today are learning the kanban system and the importance of eliminating muda (unproductive effort). You need to do so also.

The other major way you can do more with what you have is to learn and practice the minimal superset principle. Never just solve a problem: always solve at least its minimal superset so that every effort generates tools you can reuse to solve future problems. So simple. So powerful. So ignored.

While we all want success 100 percent of the time, if you never fail, you almost surely have done something wrong. Most of life is not about choosing whether or not to fail: it is choosing where. Eventually, you will have more to do than you can do, and so you are forced to choose where you fail. Recognizing this can be liberating, but another consequence is that life can be very unfair, for others after the fact may weigh your successes and failures differently than they would have at the time.

Successful people learn how to pivot, which is a nice way of saying change your mind. You need to pursue goals with single-minded dedication and focus, but periodically you also have to ask yourself whether your objectives and plans still make sense. If they do not, then you need to change and change quickly.

Finally, hone your skills of empathy. Knowing what the other party to a negotiation really wants is critical to a good outcome. Understanding what your troops hope and fear is key to leadership. Much as I stated above with respect to your own goals, people seldom are honest about what really matters to them, oftentimes because they do not really know themselves. This is where empathy matters. Put yourself in their place and be ruthlessly analytic about what you would want in a similar situation.

Advice is just that. Learning how to select good advice and ignore bad advice is perhaps one of the most basic skills of life. Do it well.

ACKNOWLEDGMENTS

THE INSPIRATION FOR THIS BOOK CAME FROM GEORGE DAY, A FRIEND OF MORE THAN FIFTY YEARS, WHOM I MET AT THE INSTITUTE FOR DEFENSE ANALYSES. He encouraged me to share my career lessons with students, so for eleven years I taught a class at the McDonough School of Business at Georgetown University, where he was then the dean. My longtime friend and colleague Nancy Hauge joined him in pushing me to do this. Naren Aryal and Brandon Coward of Amplify Publishing have been essential to completing it.

What made this book possible, though, is the many people with whom I worked over my career as customers, suppliers, colleagues, and employees, as well as those around me who tried to keep me in balance. First in this last group would be my mother, who kept clippings and items from the beginning. I once gave a speech in Brazil and wondered how my hosts were going to advertise it. They had hired a dozen women with large breasts to wear a tight T-shirt with my face in the middle and walk around the conference. Even that my mother took and kept. There was a limit. I was playing a VCR tape of a speech I had just given that included a very long introduction. Very long—like twenty minutes. She did call me back to skip that.

I hate to do special mentions because I surely am forgetting some of the many people who made me successful. With apologies to those I am forgetting, special thanks to Ken Alexander, Walter Adams, Marc Nerlove, George Eads, Hollis Chenery, Arthur Smithies, Henry Rosovsky, Fred Jewett, Jack Reardon, Bill Fitzsimmons, Melinda Varian, Harry Williams, Dick Carney, Craig Jackson, Greg George, John Lauer, Don McLagan, Chris Snyder, Joyce Rutkowski, Lelah Willoughby, Joe Dionne, Tom Sullivan, Brent Harries, Jim Savage, Eric Herr, John Bunyan, Jon Newcomb, Liz Allison, Leon Williams, Roger Levien, Lyndon Haddon, John Shoemaker, Wayland Hicks, Paul Allaire, Wayne Rosing, Eric Schmidt, Ed Zander, Joe Roebuck, Carol Bartz, Mike Morris, Ken Pelowski, Keikichi Honda, May Yip, Arun Arora, Michaele James, Bob Quinn, George Reyes, Miles Gilburne, David Colburn, Steve Case, Mike Lewis, Gil Weigand, Mike Kelly, Ted Prince, Paul Vidich, John Schanz, Matt Korn, David Gang, Gerry MacDonald, Nancy Hauge, Doug Wallace, Farrell Reynolds, Art Bilger, Brad Vaughn, Jon von Tetzchnerr, Lars Boilesson, John Cummins, Koos Bekker, Cobus Stofberg, Steve Pacak, Lord Rothermere, Martin Morgan, Paul Zwillenberg, Rob Chandhok, Joe McCollum, Peter Duffy, Hemant Shah, Kate Cassino, and many others.

I met Scott McNealy as a sophomore at Harvard and was his senior thesis advisor. We stayed in touch, and I introduced him to Doug Broyles, who hired him at Onyx, giving Scott his first job in the computer industry. As I relate in the book, he hired me into Sun, where we collaborated for over a decade.

Scott does not get nearly enough credit for his management philosophy. Sun was very well run, and when Eric Schmidt went to Google he largely copied our processes. So did others. While I usually wrote and implemented the policies, they were very often Scott's ideas. Our collaboration and friendship survive to this day.

Finally, I must acknowledge the friends and family who sustained me through this busy life. Helping me care for my mother while I traveled was key, as was giving me the balance to maintain perspective.

Thank you to all.

ABOUT THE AUTHOR

BILL RADUCHEL HAS SERVED AS A HIGH-LEVEL EXECUTIVE AND STRATEGIC ADVISER for organizations such as Sun Microsystems, AOL Time Warner, Xerox, McGraw-Hill, and the Salvation Army. Over half a century working with systems, software, and networks, he has remained at the forefront of the technology revolution in media, education, and corporate governance—including recognition at Sun as CIO of the Year and the top CTO in the computer industry, as well as CTO of the Year at AOL. He holds more than fifty issued patents, as well as a PhD in econometrics from Harvard, where he taught for five years with legendary economist John Kenneth Galbraith. He has been writing software in some form since he turned fifteen years old in 1961. He is also the author of *The New Technology State*.